Golan Heights 1967–73

Israeli Soldier

VERSUS

Syrian Soldier

COMBAT

David Campbell

First published in Great Britain in 2016 by Osprey Publishing,
PO Box 883, Oxford, OX1 9PL, UK
1385 Broadway, 5th Floor, New York, NY 10018, USA
E-mail: info@ospreypublishing.com

Osprey Publishing, part of Bloomsbury Publishing Plc

A CIP catalogue record for this book is available from the British Library

Print ISBN: 978 1 4728 1330 5
PDF ebook ISBN: 978 1 4728 1331 2
ePub ebook ISBN: 978 1 4728 1332 9

Index by Rob Munro
Typeset in Univers, Sabon and Adobe Garamond Pro
Maps by bounford.com
Originated by PDQ Media, Bungay, UK
Printed in China through World Print Ltd.

16 17 18 19 20   10 9 8 7 6 5 4 3 2 1

Osprey Publishing supports the Woodland Trust, the UK's leading
woodland conservation charity. Between 2014 and 2018 our donations
are being spent on their Centenary Woods project in the UK.

www.ospreypublishing.com

Dedication

To Sheila Urbanoski, for being decidedly more interesting than most,
and at no extra cost.

Acknowledgements

Significant thanks are due to the Israeli Government Press Office and to
Ilana Dayan, office director of the IGPO's photography department, for
her extremely generous help in sourcing many of the images used in this
book; thanks to William Jacobson of Legal Insurrection (www.
legalinsurrection.com) for his kind permission to use his image of the
trench complex at Tel A-Saki; also thanks to the staff of the Southsea
Library; to Graham Campbell for keeping the lights on; to Geoff Banks
for providing a regular excuse to abandon work and go for a cup of tea
(and because he would feel left out if he wasn't mentioned, the poor
thing); and of course to my editor Nick Reynolds, whose apparently
limitless reserves of patience continue to impress and amaze.

A note on Syrian sources

While every effort has been made to secure reliable primary and
secondary sources for this book, the current civil war that blights Syria
and its environs has made much that would have been of use with regard
to that country's military history inaccessible. As such, a greater reliance
has necessarily been put on Israeli and other international sources than
would ideally have been the case.

Editor's note

Metric measurements are used in this book. For ease of comparison
please refer to the following conversion table:

1km = 0.62 miles
1m = 1.09yd / 3.28ft / 39.37in
1cm = 0.39in
1mm = 0.04in
1kg = 2.20lb

Comparative ranks

IDF (1967)	IDF (1973)	Syrian Army	British Army
–	Rav Aluf	Feriq	Lieutenant-General
Rav Aluf	Aluf	Liwa	Major-General
Aluf	Tat Aluf	Amid	Brigadier
Aluf Mishne	Aluf Mishne	Aqid	Colonel
Sgan Aluf	Sgan Aluf	Muqaddam	Lieutenant-Colonel
Rav Seren	Rav Seren	Raid	Major
Seren	Seren	Naqib	Captain
Segen Rishon	Segen Rishon	Mulazim awwal	Lieutenant
Segen Mishne	Segen Mishne	Mulazim	Second Lieutenant
Rav Samal Rishon	Rav Samal Rishon	Mussaid awwal	Regimental Sergeant Major
Rav Samal	Rav Samal	Mussaid thani	Sergeant Major
Samal Rishon	Samal Rishon	Mussaid	Staff Sergeant
Samal	Samal	Raqib	Sergeant
Rav Turai	Rav Turai	Areef	Corporal
Turai Rishon	Turai Rishon	Jundi awwal	Lance Corporal
Turai	Turai	Jundi	Private

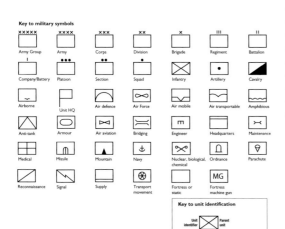

Key to military symbols

Army Group · Army · Corps · Division · Brigade · Regiment · Battalion
Company/Battery · Platoon · Section · Squad · Infantry · Artillery · Cavalry
Airborne · Unit HQ · Air defence · Air Force · Air mobile · Air transportable · Amphibious
Anti-tank · Armour · Air aviation · Bridging · Engineer · Headquarters · Maintenance
Medical · Missile · Mountain · Navy · Nuclear, biological, chemical · Ordnance · Parachute
Reconnaissance · Signal · Supply · Transport movement · Fortress or static · Fortress machine gun

Key to unit identification

Unit identifier · Parent unit · Commander · (+) with added elements (–) less elements

CONTENTS

Introduction

Though the Golan Heights was only one theatre of operations in larger wars that involved other countries on different fronts, the battles fought there by Israel and Syria in 1967 and especially 1973 were intense, uncompromising and vindictive. Ever since the creation of the State of Israel in 1948, war between this fledgling state and her neighbours, either threatened or outright, was a constant spectre. The Syrians, Jordanians, Iraqis, Lebanese and Egyptians might have made common cause against Israel in the wars up to 1967, but their individual goals, both in those earlier years as well as in the years after, were often out of sympathy with one another, driven as much by internal political concerns as by any antipathy towards the Jewish state. Such was certainly the case with Syria.

A scruffily optimistic Israeli soldier on patrol during the Six-Day War of 5–10 June 1967. Such dishevelled informality is entirely typical of many of the images of front-line Israeli troops from both the 1967 and 1973 wars; and to a degree it reflected the close-knit, informal nature of many Israeli units. (IGPO)

Since its creation in 1946 the modern Syrian state had been beset by political instability, a situation that only ended with Hafez al-Assad's seizure of power – the tenth coup in 17 years – in November 1970. For the Syrians the new state of Israel had settled on land they thought to be under their sphere of influence, with Palestine part of what some considered to be the territory of 'Greater Syria' (which also included Lebanon, Jordan and Iraq). As Syria re-established itself as a state in 1946, its belief in its own importance as a regional power owed much to its sense of itself as the historical and cultural centre of the 'fertile crescent', though it wasn't until the rise of Hafez al-Assad, a competent and pragmatic man more than an idealist, that such Pan-Syrian inclinations became an active element of Syrian policy. Until 1967 Egypt had led the Arab efforts against Israel, but by 1973 Syria, revitalized and stable, would be an equal partner in the struggle.

Added to this was a deepening enmity between the Jews and Arabs in general, and the Syrians in particular. Throughout the early and mid-1960s each side seemed to revel in the incitement of the other; regular features of this low-intensity border conflict were Israeli patrols in disputed lands, often indiscriminate shelling of Jewish settlements by Syrian artillery emplacements on the Golan, as well as cross-border incursions and tit-for-tat attacks that grew into a seemingly endless cycle of provocation, retaliation and escalation that became a material factor in the slide towards war in 1967.

The Jewish attitude to their new homeland, coloured by the still-fresh horrors of persecution in Europe as well as by the fractious and violent birth of their state, was pugnaciously defensive. At barely 480km in length and at no point wider than 130km, the physical constraints of their nation would play a pivotal role in how the Israelis approached the prospect of any conflict. Trapped as they were in a promised land surrounded by a decidedly unpromising array of implacable enemies,

A soldier of the Syrian Army poses with the Golan Heights in the background. (Photo by Miguel Pereira/Cover/Getty Images)

and with no buffer at all between those enemies and the object of their ire, the Israelis knew that because 'the lack of strategic depth made the absorption of Arab attacks on Israeli territory intolerable, Israeli operational art [would opt] for offence and first strike not only as force multipliers, but also as a means of creating artificial depth' (Kober 2011: 168). Any attack would have to knock

Women from nearby settlements serve refreshments to Israeli soldiers as they move towards the Syrian lines on the Golan Heights. (IGPO)

The main routes across the Golan were the road from Damascus that passed through Kuneitra travelling south-west through Nafekh to the Bnot Ya'acov Bridge, or a more southerly version that ran from Kuneitra to the Arik Bridge at the top of Lake Tiberias (also known as the Sea of Galilee or Lake Kinneret). A more central route passed from Damascus to the north of Kuneitra through Hamadiya where it crossed into the Golan, running between the Israel Defense Forces (IDF) positions on Hermonit to the north and 'Booster' to the south, continuing westwards to Gonen in Israel. A road also runs alongside the Trans-Arabian Pipeline, more commonly known as the Tapline, which crosses the Golan Heights from north-west to south-east (from Lebanon all the way down to Bahrain). The Israelis had a string of strongpoints supported by tanks all along the Purple Line (the United Nations-mandated 1967 ceasefire zone between Israel and Syria along the Golan, so-called because of its purple colour on UN maps), and had also dug an anti-tank ditch along the whole length of the border with Syria.

their opponent off balance from the very first, because only in such a situation could the Israelis hope to create a battlespace that wasn't on their own doorstep.

The Arab view that 'greater Israel, though illegal, is considered indispensable for the security of smaller Israel' (el Badri et al. 1978: 4) would probably find ready agreement among many Israelis. Israel's pre-emptive seizure of Arab lands in the Sinai and Golan would solve to a fair degree the strategic need for a buffer zone, but it was (and in the case of the Golan Heights remains) poisonous politically. By winning strategic breathing space in 1967 the Israelis would, to some degree, become the authors of their continuing misfortune; certainly the loss of such lands was a sharp and continuing humiliation for both Egypt and Syria, making any sort of rapprochement exceedingly unlikely, and the war in 1973 all but inevitable. In six years the state of Israel went from what looked like one of the most decisive military victories in the annals of warfare to a desperate struggle with those selfsame enemies that, if lost, would have threatened the very existence of the nation. For both Israelis and Syrians the potent psychological impact of the battles for the Golan Heights would redefine how they saw themselves – and their enemies – for decades to come.

Israeli armour coping with difficult terrain on the Golan Heights during the Six-Day War. This picture gives a good indication of how troublesome the landscape of the Golan could be for mechanized warfare; by turns barren, rough, rocky and treacherous, shot through with gullies, defiles and any number of other natural obstacles, as well as being peppered with loose volcanic rocks, the environment would prove to be punishing on both Israeli and Syrian vehicles and men. The light tank in the foreground is a French-made and -supplied AMX-13. Though not well armoured, the AMX-13 had a 75mm gun (a derivative of the German 7.5cm KwK 42 L/70) which had been a match for the Arab armour of earlier wars but fared less well in 1967 against Soviet-supplied T-54 main battle tanks. (IGPO)

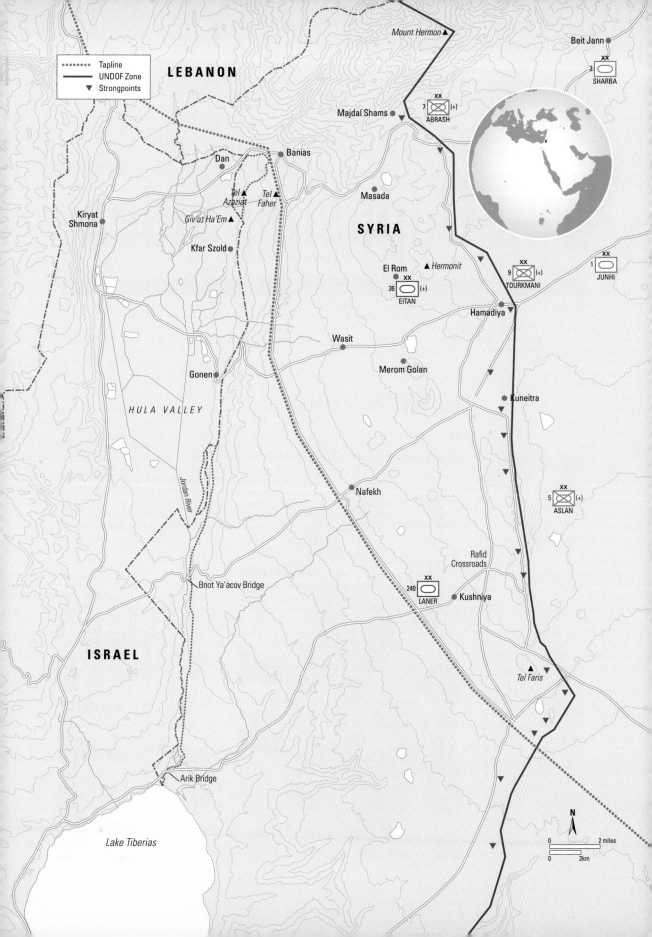

The Opposing Sides

ORIGINS AND ETHOS

Israeli

An Israeli soldier cleans his 7.62mm FN FAL *Romat* (short for *Rov've Mittan*, or 'self-loading') battle rifle during the War of Attrition, 1970. For most of its existence the IDF had operated under the ideology of *Ein breira* or 'no alternative', the basis of which was that for Israel to lose a war was the equivalent of losing the entire state. Up until the 1982 war in Lebanon there was much truth in such an idea, where soldiers knew that they were fighting for their homes and families in a literal, rather than figurative sense. There are plenty of anecdotes of men being close enough to their homes that they could see their neighbourhoods or settlements from where they fought. The impetus to win that such immediate and vital connections provoked cannot be underestimated, and was certainly a factor in the success of the IDF as a cohesive fighting force. (IGPO)

The Israel Defense Forces (IDF) developed from a blend of the Israelis' military experiences of both conventional and unconventional warfare together with an understanding that, for a more formally constituted force, Israel's limited manpower resources required a central cadre of professional officers and NCOs surrounded by an active-duty conscript force, backed up with 'a large body of standing reserves' (Gal 1986: 11) that, if fully activated, would comprise 'well over 10% of the total Jewish population, the highest mobilisation ratio in modern times' (Rothenberg 1979: 57). Israel's unique problems – the proximity of its enemies, its inability to conduct any sort of defence in depth, and the impossibility of sustaining conflict for any period of time due to scarce

resources and limited manpower – stimulated the development of a particular approach to combat operations: the IDF would need to be highly aggressive to deter potential attackers, flexible in attack and defence, able to carry the war into the enemy's territory, and most importantly to be decisive, bringing any conflict to a speedy and definite conclusion before the strain on the infrastructure of the state became too severe.

The fact that Israel was a state born out of struggle contributed to the mindset of Israelis that one fights, rather than negotiates, for victory. Lieutenant Colonel Avigdor Kahalani, commander of the 77th Armored Battalion during the ferocious battle in the Valley of Tears in October 1973, noted how 'Our doctrine believes that the best defense is a good offense. Most of our training was on how to attack. Our ideology preaches that if you attack, you have more of a chance for success. Israeli tacticians teach that you really can't achieve a victory through defense, so it was not emphasized in our service schools' (quoted in Prosch 1979: 6). Such aggression was married to forces that were highly mobile and which were led by men who were clever, flexible and free from the hidebound practices of more conventionally educated armies.

Thus for the IDF, mobility and flexibility would become a defining operational approach. An unnamed Israeli officer described it thus:

> With the exception of the bunkers and village defensive positions, the entire Israeli defensive force was capable of movement. Tanks, self-propelled artillery, infantry and armoured infantry were all in motion or could be at short notice. Artillery batteries moved set-up, fired, rested, moved and fired again within minutes of receiving an order … the entire firepower of the Israeli battle force could move from one fulcrum to another in an infinite variety of combinations. An attacker could never be certain just what combination he might encounter. It was a strategy based on mobility and the paramount Israeli requirement that the expense in men and equipment be minimal. (Quoted in Dunstan 2008: 28)

Such a war of movement would be richly rewarded in the Six-Day War of 1967, during which it seemed that the Israeli forces could do little wrong, though there were problems apparent for those who chose to look. The gap 'between the great importance of the operational level, on the one hand, and the almost nonexistent formal military thinking invested in it on the other' (Kober 2011: 169) would contribute to the unbalancing of Israeli forces in favour of armour in the succeeding years – a policy that would display its shortcomings all too soon.

Syrian

The most important fact to understand about the Syrian armed forces of the time is that they were, first and foremost, a political entity, even more so than in other Arab countries. Since the formation of the modern Syrian state in 1946, the Syrian Army had gradually become little more than a political plaything for the factions and strongmen who used it as a means to dictatorial ends; 'Indeed, by the 1950s, most young officers were joining the army expressly as a means of gaining political power' (Pollack 2004: 457). Its military duties always came a poor second to the factionalism and internecine strife that infected all levels of the Syrian political system.

The Syrian Army had been founded by France, ruler of the newly created mandates of Syria and Lebanon, in the wake of World War I. Established in 1919 as the *Troupes spéciales du Levant*, this force was rarely called on for any sort of strenuous duty, so the army of the newly independent state of Syria that went to war in 1948 was a fairly ramshackle affair of 12,000 men mostly grouped in three infantry brigades and a battalion-size armoured force.

A Syrian Arab carrying a 9mm MP 40 submachine gun leaps over a wall while receiving covering fire from the dismally unreliable French 8mm Chauchat light machine gun, near Jerusalem, Palestine, 17 April 1948. The combination of French and German weapons was a legacy of Syria's recent past as a protectorate of France; weapons and equipment of every type were in short supply, so surplus matériel from Europe, including pre-war Renault R 35 light infantry tanks and a variety of small arms, were eagerly sought after. The Syrian Army was founded by the French in 1919 as the *Troupes spéciales du Levant*, a force that would form the bases of both future Syrian and Lebanese armies, though it was never expected to do very much, the historian Kenneth Pollack noting how 'Paris had relied primarily on French regulars to keep the peace in Syria and had neglected indigenous forces. Consequently, training was lackadaisical, discipline lax, and staff work almost unheard of. In terms of quantitative strength there were about 12,000 men in the Syrian army. These troops were mostly grouped into three infantry brigades and an armored force of about battalion size' (Pollack 2004: 448). (Photo by PhotoQuest/ Getty Images)

Nevertheless, there was much to be said for their bravery and for the general cohesiveness of their units 'even under intense pressure' (Pollack 2004: 455). The more complicated aspects of warfighting, such as combined-arms operations, proved less successful, especially when there hadn't been time for intensive planning beforehand. That lack of initiative was also apparent in manoeuvring, where lack of preparation would usually lead to costly and often unsuccessful frontal assaults. When all was said and done their performance during the 1948–49 war was not as disastrous as that of some of their co-combatants, with Syrian troops often proving brave and stubborn, better suited to defensive rather than offensive operations.

Syria's president, Hafez al-Assad, is pictured in the uniform of a general officer on 27 October 1973. In the expectation of a new war with Israel Assad understood that things had to change if he was to stand any chance of defeating the Israelis. To that end he made two significant decisions: 'First, he would have to set aside his well-developed sense of paranoia and turn the military into a more professional (and thus less politically reliable) force. Second, he would have to strike a deal with the Soviets – whom he never trusted – for weapons, training and expertise' (Pollack 2004: 479). This second decision bore better fruit than Assad might have at first imagined thanks to Egypt, which, in 1972, expelled the majority of its Soviet advisors, leaving the way clear for Damascus to become the Soviet Union's most important ally in the Middle East. (AFP/Getty Images)

Though they were not of the same calibre as the more professional British-officered Jordanians, there was no reason to suppose that Syria's armed forces could not develop in a similar fashion; but the succeeding decades would prove to be poisonous for the effectiveness of the Syrian Army, consumed by domestic issues. In the years immediately after 1948, France continued to be Syria's main supplier of weaponry, with large amounts of German war surplus (from small arms to the PzKpfw IV medium tanks that would have a second a life guarding the Golan) finding its way into the hands of the nascent force. The evolving nature of the region's politics (led by Egypt's resurgent Pan-Arabic nationalism) meant that old colonial ties withered, however, replaced from the mid-1950s onwards by the Soviets, who brought a new military doctrine and, eventually, the weapons to implement it.

Assad made full use of his new ally's generosity, though the planning for the 1973 war, albeit carried out in accordance with Soviet doctrine, was a Syrian project with relatively little input from Moscow's advisors; it was highly detailed and specific, with great attention paid to the roles and objectives of every participating unit. It had its failings: the Syrian planners probably didn't have the experience to adapt the Soviet blueprint of an armoured attack designed for central Europe to the distinctive, difficult terrain of the Golan; and the reaction of the Israelis to such an attack seems to have been given little consideration, with an assumption that they would just 'play their part'. Nevertheless, the scope, ambition and strength of the undertaking augured well for success.

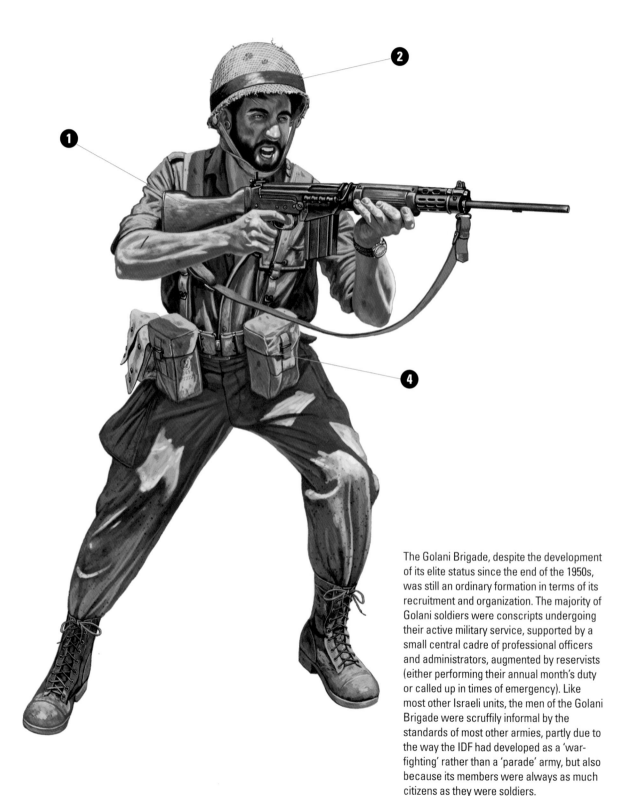

The Golani Brigade, despite the development of its elite status since the end of the 1950s, was still an ordinary formation in terms of its recruitment and organization. The majority of Golani soldiers were conscripts undergoing their active military service, supported by a small central cadre of professional officers and administrators, augmented by reservists (either performing their annual month's duty or called up in times of emergency). Like most other Israeli units, the men of the Golani Brigade were scruffily informal by the standards of most other armies, partly due to the way the IDF had developed as a 'war-fighting' rather than a 'parade' army, but also because its members were always as much citizens as they were soldiers.

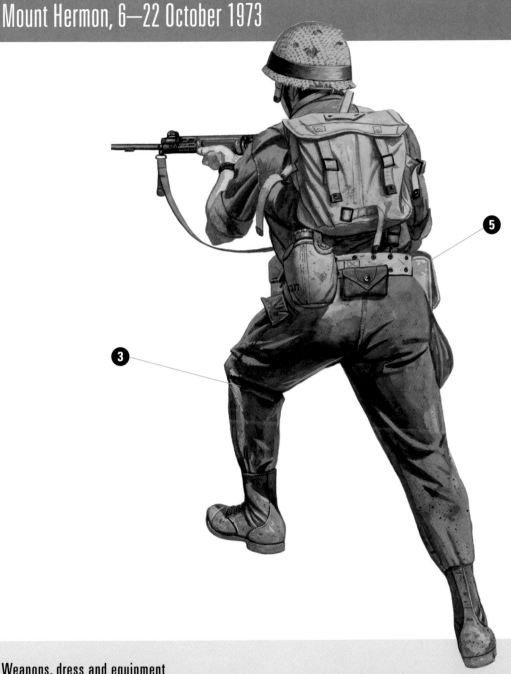

Weapons, dress and equipment

The Israeli carries a 7.62mm FN FAL battle rifle (**1**) known as the *Romat* (short for *Rov've Mittan*, or 'self-loading'), an Israeli version that was more or less the same as other FN models, chambered for 7.62×51mm NATO rounds; the rifle used 20-round magazines and was semi-automatic, the full-automatic option being found on the heavy-barrelled squad support version. The *Romat* was serviceable but not terribly popular, especially with APC-borne troops who found its 109cm length rather burdensome.

He wears an M1 helmet (**2**) covered with the ubiquitous mesh netting secured with a strip of roughly-cut black rubber. His battledress (**3**) is olive-coloured and is notable for the tight cut of the

trousers (called *Taibas* pants), a fashion choice that started among truck drivers and warehouse workers that quickly spread to become common throughout the IDF of the period.

He carries two ammunition pouches (**4**) based on the British 58-pattern style that each held two FN FAL magazines, a grenade pouch (**5**) capable of carrying two grenades, a backpack and a water bottle on Israeli-made webbing – it was the Israeli habit to adapt existing patterns of webbing and uniform to their own specification and manufacture them within Israel. His average combat load would be around 15–20kg, though it could be considerably more (up to 40kg) when operating independently of armoured personnel carriers.

RECRUITMENT, MORALE AND LOGISTICS

Israeli

Within Israeli society military service was (and still is) almost universal, widely understood and accepted. From the outset the state was defined by its ability to sustain itself through war to the point that 'there was an inseparable connection between the political, social and economic aspects of the Jewish community and the development of military strength' (Rothenberg 1979: 14). To be an Israeli is, perforce, to be a soldier. For most armies such a reliance on reservists is an unwelcome necessity due to the difficulties of maintaining discipline, readiness and cohesion in such a force, but as Martin van Creveld notes, the opposite seems to have been the case for the Israelis:

> The reserve units experience little personnel turbulence, so the men who constitute them remain together for many years on end. Meeting regularly for maintenance, training, and operational service, they form extremely cohesive units – complete with all the shared worldview, bonhomie, and mutual aid that implies. For example, during the June 1967 war some of the personnel forming the armored ugda (division) in the center of Israel's Egyptian front had served together for five or six years. (Creveld 2002: 115)

Such strong cultural cohesion was amplified by the informal nature of much of the IDF, as well as the trust the men had in their officers at almost every level. Avigdor Kahalani noted that 'Everybody fights first to save his own life. But the second most important reason why soldiers will fight is because they are told to by their commander. If they believe in their commander, they will

fight for him. Without this feeling, nobody will fight' (quoted in Prosch 1979: 10). Reserve units were also wedded to their vehicles and equipment, and were responsible for all storage and upkeep. In this manner when a reserve formation was called up it would have familiar, working tanks, armoured personnel carriers (APCs) and trucks at the unit's depot, ready for immediate use.

Supplies might have been limited, but the cartoonist Bill Mauldin, in Israel during the 1967 war, noticed that

> It is a Spartan army, brought into being under Spartan circumstances. But it's not a hardship army. The men and women get their mail regularly, and they have PXs of a sort dispensing soft drinks, tobacco and a few other luxuries … The army's food is simple but substantial, the boots are rugged but fit, the uniforms are faded but mended. The morale is tremendous. Combine all this with masterful leadership and you have a military machine that can take on its weight in wildcats. (Mauldin 1968: 337)

The timely supply of units in the field was recognized as a point of friction by the logistics branch; by operating in a strongly aggressive and highly mobile manner, Israeli armoured forces – traditionally fantastically fuel- and ammunition-hungry – would find the impact of their assaults blunted because they would have to pause as supplies were called up. Therefore,

> During the mid-1960s, the IDF underwent major logistical reform. From then on, divisions or brigades were directly in charge of 'pushing' supplies to their own forces along the lines of operation. The motivation to do so was high, the communication lines were relatively short, and personal acquaintances between the providers of supplies and the fighting forces made the mission simpler. (Kober 2011: 176)

A soldier receives first aid in the field. The Israelis took considerable care to look after their wounded and their dead, as observed by the historian Barbara Tuchman: 'No aspect of the IDF is more striking than its concern for casualties. Every man wounded or dead is brought back regardless of cost, even that of mounting an offensive to recover the missing. In most cases the wounded were in hospitals within an hour, transported directly from the place they fell by helicopter, and the knowledge of this was a strong morale factor' (quoted in Gal 1986: 236). The urge to do one's duty, no matter the cost, was very strong in the IDF, as described by the historian Samuel Rolbant: 'Men said what worried them most was what others would think of them, or what their friends and families would feel about them when they came home. The vague fear of shame, of possible ostracism or disapproval they might experience on getting home alive unscathed, featured prominently in the boys' answers about their behaviour on the battlefield. Everybody knew where you were, in what outfit you served, what you did or failed to do, so that it was imperative to return with a clean bill of moral health, morality in this case being judged by standards of selflessness' (quoted in Gal 1986: 149). (IGPO)

Syrian

Syrian soldiers surrender on the Golan, 1973. Repeated accounts of battles in 1967 and throughout 1973 give testament to the personal bravery and competence of the average Syrian soldier, who would prove to be uncommonly stubborn, especially in defence. The tactical shortcomings of such men, either in armoured or combined-arms combat, must be laid by and large at the door of their officers, who, though far from universally poor, were themselves more often than not badly trained in the handling of their troops. Such deficiencies were due in part to the lack of a strong professional tradition within the army, as well as the difficulties – which should not be underestimated – of taking the semi-professional mostly infantry force of 1967 and turning it, in a little over three years, into a fully mechanized force of five divisions armed with modern weaponry, which was supplied in conjunction with a doctrine honed for a different theatre of operations against a different kind of enemy. (IPGO)

Soldiers in the Syrian Army could not fail to be aware of the ethical and cultural currents that were sweeping through the broader society of Syria; the Ba'ath Party had come to power in 1963, bringing with it a confusing mix of nationalistic, anti-imperial, socialist ideas, but more importantly it brought in a generation of men (like Hafez al-Assad) who had a pragmatic approach to the consolidation of power. The armed forces had traditionally been a stronghold of the urban Sunni community, but after 1963 a series of purges saw such men replaced by Alawites, Druze and Ismailis from more rural backgrounds – men with familial and cultural loyalty to the Ba'ath Party leadership in Damascus. More than ever the Syrian Army was a route of opportunity to sections of the populace who had traditionally been on the back foot, though that opportunity was not so much for a professional military career as it was nakedly political: in the run-up to the 1967 war over 2,000 officers were purged to make way for newer, more politically reliable blood. Though the new preponderance of such men, from different ethnic and religious backgrounds to those of their mostly Sunni troops, had the potential to exacerbate fault lines between the two, the historian Kenneth Pollack asserts that: 'While there is no evidence to support the specific contention of sectarian problems, there is ample evidence that Syrian officers generally neglected their troops' (Pollack 2004: 470).

The average Syrian soldier seems in most cases to have been tough and effective on an individual level. Made up of mostly rural conscripts from a range of ethnic backgrounds, the Syrian Army, despite its radical programme of change between 1967 and 1973, continued to rely heavily upon such solid, stubborn men for the bulk of its troops. The Syrian soldier of 1967 often proved to be a tough, tenacious fighter, especially in defence, and such courage was also to be a feature in the Yom Kippur War of 1973, with a general

A Syrian soldier in an orchard, looking rather more like a farmer, wearing a *keffiyeh* (Arab headdress) and carrying a Czech-built Vz. 52 semi-automatic rifle, 20 October 1973, a few days before the end of the war. The man's casual dress and his old-fashioned rifle make him likely to be some form of local militiaman. The Syrian invasion that had been launched barely 14 days previously had ground to a halt in less than a week, with rapid Israeli counter-attacks driving deep into Syrian territory. The panic caused by the IDF's advances was by this stage mitigating somewhat, in part because its advance had stalled (a combination of being overstretched and the timely arrival of the Iraqis to soak up some of the Israelis' firepower), and also because both sides knew that a ceasefire was fast-approaching. The Syrians would not need to consider trying to implement the sort of general mobilization that was, for Israel, the difference between survival and complete defeat. (Photo by Hulton Archive/Getty Images)

acknowledgement that, leadership failings aside, most of the men fought creditably. British journalist Charles Wakebridge was of the opinion that

> The soldiers and junior officers fought well in battle and bravely, but they could have been better led by their middle-grade and senior officers and better directed by a hesitant, indecisive and perhaps uncomprehending general headquarters. One senses a feeling of bitterness by the soldiers and junior leaders against their seniors. An Israeli brigadier who fought on the Golan, to whom I spoke, gave his verdict that the Syrian infantry fought with considerable courage and were better equipped and trained than in 1967 … His opinion of the ability and performance of Syrian officers was not high. (Wakebridge 1976: 30)

In a similar vein, Kenneth Pollack notes that 'Although Syrian divisions and brigades were often shattered by Israeli penetrations and flanking maneuvers, the smaller formations – platoons, companies, and even battalions – maintained their cohesiveness and either stood their ground and fought until overcome or retreated as intact units. Moreover, they generally conducted fighting withdrawals rather than fleeing' (Pollack 2004: 509).

LEADERSHIP AND COMMUNICATIONS

Israeli

From the outset of the State of Israel's establishment, the importance of good leadership has been understood. Reuven Gal states that 'The IDF leadership has been traditionally characterized by adventurous officers instead of cautious NCOs, leading from the front instead of issuing orders from the rear, demonstrating improvisation, initiative and flexibility rather than going by the book, and showing a sense of duty and commitment rather than career considerations' (Gal 1986: 115). That such leadership was highly individual, and generally the better for it, is illustrated in numerous recollections, such as those of Avigdor Kahalani. On being asked how he kept his battalion operational when outnumbered 10 to 1, Kahalani stated that 'the key thing is leadership. Your units will be cohesive and will stay together if they believe in their leaders. Everybody has their own style of leadership and how to do this. If your unit follows you and you are successful, then your style is all right. The main thing is that it works' (quoted in Prosch 1979: 6).

The informality and close-knit nature of the men within their units – the sense of all being in it together – also played a factor. Added to this was the soldier's knowledge that every officer had been where he was, for there was no separate 'officer corps' as such in the IDF; all officers had been NCOs, and regular conscripts prior to that, with their selection for promotion and officer training based upon proven ability and potential.

Command in the IDF was largely decentralized, with a great deal of responsibility, as well as freedom of action, given to relatively junior officers. The defining ethos that drove such men was one of personal action, never asking their men to do something that they would not, leading them by example behind the lines and from the front in the attack; 'And so, since all commanders' training in the IDF is geared towards this moment of charging the enemy, the dictum "A'harye" (the Hebrew word for "follow me") is imprinted in all junior commanders from their earliest training' (Gal 1986: 135). The harmonica player Larry Adler, in Israel to entertain the troops during the Six-Day War, witnessed this ethos in practice for himself:

> There are many reasons why rank is almost abandoned but one main one why military efficiency still works, and it is something I heard many times. The Israeli officer doesn't say, 'Forward,' he says 'Follow me.' Which is why the majority of casualties were among officers and it helps to understand why no grade of soldier in the Israeli Army can be a second-class citizen. (Adler 1968: 338)

The workhorse of infantry communications was the AN/PRC-25, the back-borne American radio set that had gained extensive use in Vietnam. All M3 half-tracks carried a radio, though the sets could be original SCR 509s or SCR 510s, old British Mk 9 Wireless sets, or any number of other potential makes; battalion-level communications in the Golani Brigade were all managed through a dedicated communications M3 half-track that would liaise with the brigade net, also housed in a specially converted 'command' M3. Such command vehicles were often expressions of the needs and personalities of the

men who commanded from them, and as such tended to vary widely. Though Israeli communications were generally good they suffered from situational problems, for example at Tel Faher, where the loss of communications between brigade and battalion, and also between battalion and company, led to additional casualties. These would include the commanding officer of the 12th Battalion, killed when he went to see with his own eyes what the radios had been unable to transmit.

Syrian

As mentioned above, the Syrian Army was an entirely political entity, its focus being the maintenance of domestic control rather than the defeat of foreign enemies. In addition, the numerous coups and countercoups that dominated Syria throughout this period were always 'followed by a purge of the officer corps in which the victor would attempt to extirpate all of the loser's supporters from the ranks. Invariably, these purges fell heaviest on the senior officers, whose ranks were decimated by the end of the 1950s' (Pollack 2004: 458). Such a toll certainly played a part in the generally poor performance of the Syrians in the Six-Day War, though the relative stability offered by Assad's coup in November 1970 helped to alleviate the situation somewhat, even if it didn't change the nature of the beast.

In the field the calibre of the Syrian infantry officer from platoon level upwards left much to be desired. They were poorly trained and for the most part lacked any sense of initiative or personal flair, often failing in the most basic of military tasks. Perhaps even more seriously, and in strong contrast to the Israelis, Syrian officers seemed to have little interest in or care for the men under their command, a case in point being the denouement of the Six-Day War where an erroneous Syrian radio broadcast stating that Kuneitra had fallen led to the widespread collapse of the Syrian Army, with examples of officers abandoning their men and racing back to Damascus in their staff cars.

COMBAT

A Syrian paratrooper from Lieutenant Ahmed
Rifai al-Joju's A Company charges across the
slopes of Mount Hermon after his company's
insertion by helicopter on 6 October 1973.
He is equipped in the usual fashion of a
Syrian infantryman, though he wears a
home-grown version of the old French 'lizard'
pattern camouflage uniform. The average
Syrian soldier, though still a conscript, was
better trained and equipped, if not
necessarily better led, in 1973 than in 1967.
The officers and men of the 82nd Paratroop
and 183rd Commando battalions were a
different matter, however. The Syrian Army
had developed along decidedly Soviet lines
in the years since 1967, with one facet of
such close cooperation being that the
officers of elite Syrian units – including the
82nd – received specialist tactical training in
the Soviet Union. Such officers led their men
with competence and initiative, ensuring that
their troops were experienced in a variety of
missions and tactical roles that were beyond
the majority of the Syrian Army rank and file.

Weapons, dress and equipment

This soldier carries a 7.62mm AKM assault rifle (**1**), an upgraded version of the 7.62mm AK-47 assault rifle that was lighter and easier to manufacture, and which fired a 7.62×39mm cartridge. The AKM used 30-round magazines and could fire either in semi- or full-automatic modes.

He wears a Soviet Ssh-60 helmet (**2**) with mesh netting. He also wears a non-regulation *keffiyeh* headdress (**3**) which would have been welcome in the low temperatures experienced on the Golan and Mount Hermon during the month of October.

His equipment is supported by leather Y-straps (**4**) identical to those issued to Soviet motorized infantry in the 1960s apart from the belt (**5**), which is a British Pattern 37 model common among Syrian infantry in both the 1967 and 1973 wars. He carries a grenade pouch (**6**) suitable for two F1 'Limonka'-type grenades, an ammunition pouch (**7**) capable of carrying three magazines for his AKM as well as a rifle cleaning kit, a Type II bayonet (**8**) with its distinctive moulded red plastic sheath, and a gasmask bag (**9**). His combat load comes to around 20kg, though this would increase to 25–30kg with the addition of a backpack when operating away from fixed positions or vehicles.

A group of Iraqi officers meet with General Ahmad Suedani (fourth from the left), the Syrian Chief of Staff, on 6 June 1967. Kenneth Pollack, though he has some good things to say about several of the divisional commanders, sees the failings of Syria's military leaders in the 1973 war as severe, but not entirely fatal: 'Syria's strategic leadership, its divisional commanders and above, performed very unevenly. In some ways they were quite good and were a principal element of the successes the Syrians enjoyed in the war. In other ways they were miserable and contributed to the overall defeat of Syrian arms. On balance, however, they did as much good as harm and cannot be considered the decisive element in Syria's military failure' (Pollack 2004: 502). Decent planning was blunted by hesitation and indecision in moments that called for boldness and clarity, failures were reinforced and successes were often left unexploited, but it would be the tactical failings of the Syrian Army that would prove most deadly to their hopes of victory. (AFP/Getty Images)

The rise of Hafez al-Assad led to a rebalancing of the officer corps, with the worst of the political hacks and timeservers shown the door; but despite moves towards a more merit-based system of promotion in junior and middle ranks, the higher echelons were still ruthlessly political. Soviet doctrine and training gave the officers of the refashioned Syrian Army clear roles and responsibilities, but it was probably too much to expect that the entire character of the organization could be transformed in such a short time. While there is no doubt that the average Syrian officer was now more competent in the execution of his duties, the determination of the limits of those duties had not changed: the rigid hierarchy, the fear – indeed active discouragement – of any sort of independent action not sanctioned by a higher authority, and the rote practising of drills and manoeuvres, encouraged and rewarded inflexibility and denied the value of independent thought. Such rigidity could be accommodated when, as in the earliest phases of the October 1973 attack, the officers leading companies, battalions and brigades had detailed and specific orders to follow; but when the combat environment changed, as it inevitably did, such officers often found themselves at a loss, paralysed by indecision and unable to adapt to deviations from their highly practised routines.

Tight command and control was a feature of Soviet operational art, and one way in which this manifested itself was the proliferation of radios throughout mechanized formations. This approach, together with the equipment that facilitated it, was a feature of the Soviet Union's re-armament of Syria after 1970. Divisional, regimental, battalion and company radio nets were deployed; company commanders would each have an R-113 and an R-105 radio mounted in their vehicle, as well as an R-126 portable radio. Platoon leaders had R-113s in their vehicles as well as an R-126 for use when dismounted; each squad APC would have an R-113, though the squad leaders had no portable radio sets. Syrian communications were perhaps not all they could have been, however, with the Israelis scoring a number of intelligence successes due to poor radio discipline, and radio nets also could not make up for the systemic problems that beset the Syrian officer corps.

ARMAMENT, TRAINING AND TACTICS

Israeli

Great stock was put in the teachings of men like Orde Wingate and especially Basil Liddell Hart; the latter's 'books and articles emphasized less expensive ways of winning offensively, primarily with quality rather than quantity' (Weller 1974: 19). Yigael Yadin, commanding officer of the Haganah Officer's School (1940–43), was a strong proponent of Liddell Hart's training books (for example *Infantry Training, Small Arms Training*): 'What Liddell Hart taught was exactly what we needed. We were and are a small nation; we must win quickly at a minimum of cost. We need especially to take maximum advantage of surprise, mobility, and quality. It's easier and cheaper to defeat our enemies from the flank, and rear than by ponderous frontal attacks' (quoted in Weller 1974: 13).

Avigdor Kahalani's view echoed the Liddell Hart doctrine by acknowledging that, lacking numbers, a different approach was needed: 'Our philosophy is that we would rather have a few very qualified soldiers than a large number of mediocre or average soldiers. We train our soldiers to a high degree of readiness. Because of our lack of a large population base for a large army, we are forced to adopt this philosophy of quality rather than quantity' (quoted in Prosch 1979: 6).

By 1967 the IDF, although recognizably more professional than the force that fought the wars of 1956 and especially 1948–49, was still under-equipped and operating within tight operational margins. Bill Mauldin commented that

> Israeli forces are made up mostly of farmers, home-builders and merchants who have had a long and gaunt struggle for survival. As a result, the army itself can operate on a shoestring. By US standards, Israel's troops are incredibly frugal. Left behind is none of the postbattle debris you expect from almost any other army: thrown-away packs, gas masks, broken weapons, bandoliers of ammunition, cases of grenades, half-used rations, bits of clothing, web equipment, and so forth. Israelis don't have stuff to throw away, so they don't throw it. (Mauldin 1968: 335)

Despite such shortcomings there was an appreciation that the basic approach the Israelis were forced to adopt had the advantage of forcing them to become more adaptable and creative; the American military observer James Metcalfe noted that 'the Israeli soldier ... had taught military men a valuable lesson: one should not "place so much reliance on push-button gadgets that we forget the importance of the little man with the little rifle"' (quoted in Rothenberg 1979: 66).

Such trust in 'the little man with the little rifle' seemed to diminish somewhat in the wake of the armoured successes of the 1967 war. The historian and journalist Jac Weller, interviewing British General Staff officers who had met some of the Israeli commanders in the wake of their victory, noted their rather cold opinion of their guests: 'Israeli armor officers think they are still living in a horse cavalry environment and believe they can do it all with tanks alone. The IDF officer refuses to recognize that the combined arms team of tanks, infantry, and artillery is an essential to winning, even for survival on the modern battlefield' (quoted in Weller 1977: 4).

Israeli soldiers on the Hermon, mid-October 1973. The men shown here are dressed and equipped in an entirely typical fashion. The 9mm Uzi submachine gun first saw widespread use in the Six-Day War and was favoured by paratroopers and mechanized infantry alike for its compact nature and reliability, despite its limited range. The soldier to the right carries the squad-support version of the FN FAL *Romat*, a lightly modified Israeli version of the ubiquitous FN FAL battle rifle, with the squad-support version different only in its use of a heavier barrel and bipod. This weapon was never terribly popular, in part due to its extra weight as well as a limited capacity to lay down sustained fire because of its reliance upon the same 20-round box-magazine feed system as the *Romat*. (IGPO)

The enormity of the victory in 1967 would lead to a clear over-reliance on armoured formations over any other – a fault that would cost the Israelis dearly both in Egypt and on the Golan in 1973, when the ratio of tanks to APCs had risen to 3:1. A common view at this time was that 'Infantry in the IDF is only a stepsister to "armor" and a weak one at that. IDF "armor" and "paratrooper" officers seem to consider "infantry" almost like militia' (Weller 1977: 5). The infantry contingents of armoured units were reduced, leaving tank-heavy forces that would prove vulnerable to well-planned Egyptian and Syrian defensive tactics. Jac Weller noted the snobbery within the IDF's armoured units, still present four years after the Yom Kippur War of October 1973: '"Armor" in the IDF does include riflemen and machinegunners in APCs. But, even when they dismount to fight on foot, they are still "armor." Nobody doubts that the number of riflemen and machinegunners in "armor"

An Israeli half-track on patrol in the lead-up to the Six-Day War. This particular vehicle is an M3A1 Mark 'B', which differs from the Mark 'A' standard troop-carrier version because of the addition of an armoured ring mount, which in this case bears a .30-calibre Browning medium machine gun instead of the more common .50-calibre M2HB Browning heavy machine gun. The Israelis used any number of American half-tracks sourced over a number of years and in a variety of ways. (IGPO)

An Israeli artillery crew in the act of firing a 175mm M107 long-range self-propelled gun, known as the *Romach* ('Spear') in IDF service, on the Golan front, 11 October 1973. Though it had a slow rate of fire – only one or two rounds per minute – the gun had considerable range (34km), meaning that its rounds, which weighed 67kg each, could traverse the entire width of the Golan Heights and hit the Syrian Army's jumping-off points, its main axis of travel and its surface-to-air missile (SAM) air-defence network. Despite such potential the artillery force was something of a Cinderella service within the IDF; it had a higher proportion of self-propelled guns (including the 155mm M109) than towed guns, in accordance with the Israeli obsession with mobile warfare, but lacked numbers of both types, the force being comprised of just three artillery brigades to cover all fronts at the time of the Yom Kippur War in October 1973. In contrast, the five Syrian Army divisions that made up the attacking force in October 1973 had over 950 artillery pieces – both integral to the divisions and in dedicated artillery regiments – in support of their attack on the Golan alone. (IGPO)

has increased since 1973, but every man still wears the black beret' (Weller 1977: 6). Six years after the hard lessons of the Yom Kippur War, Avigdor Kahalani was still wedded to the dream of armour as his nation's defining military tool: 'We believe that the tank can continue to protect our country. We feel the tank is better than any other unit or any other equipment on the ground' (quoted in Prosch 1979: 8).

Syrian

Beginning in 1958, a few years after Egypt had gone down the same path, the Syrians began seeking military assistance from Moscow, first in equipment and then later in advisors. The Syrian Army – initially little more than a French-fashioned police force – had little in the way of learned doctrine or military success that could inform the way that it understood and adapted to the Soviet way of doing things. 'The Syrians, although somewhat reluctantly and perhaps in the absence of any of their own, seemed to have accepted without question Soviet military doctrines, evolved in World War II with Europe and Stalingrad very much in mind but without modification on adaption to local conditions, needs and resources' (Wakebridge 1976: 28).

The disasters of the 1967 campaign led to a wholesale reinvention of the Syrian Army from 1970 onwards, leading to it being rebuilt from the ground up in the modern Soviet fashion, with tank and mechanized divisions using tables of organization and equipment that closely mirrored their Russian counterparts. Large numbers of Soviet advisors and specialists were detailed to Syria (somewhere around 3,000 in all by 1973) and 'were attached to every Syrian combat formation down to battalion and squadron level' (Pollack 2004: 481). In particular, the Russians spent a great deal of time instructing their charges on the use of the new weapons systems that were being made available to them, including the SAM-6 and ZSU-23-4 anti-aircraft systems, T-62 main battle tank, 9M14 *Malyutka* (AT-3) anti-tank guided missile (ATGM) and RPG-7 shoulder-launched anti-tank rocket-propelled grenade

Two Syrian Army soldiers keep watch in Damascus during the last throes of the Yom Kippur War, 24 October 1973. The *keffiyeh*-wearing man on the left holds a Soviet-built 7.62mm PPSh-41 submachine gun and the one on the right holds a Czech-built 7.62mm Vz. 52 semi-automatic rifle; a Czech-built 7.62mm Vz. 52 machine gun lies at their feet. Damascus was the preserve of troops like the Presidential Guard – units that were in the charge of close friends or family members of President Assad and thus absolutely loyal to the regime. In consequence such troops tended to have the smartest uniforms, the best tanks and APCs, and all the newest Soviet small arms. The fact that such well-armed and -equipped men were needed desperately at the front was a moot point, for with a police state the most important consideration, over and above the winning and losing of wars, is its own security and survival. (Photo by Hulton Archive/Getty Images)

launcher. In general the Soviet systems were designed 'down' to the level of the average soldier, and such a democratic approach certainly helped the Syrians adapt to their new equipment quickly – indeed, the Israelis thought Syrian tank crews they encountered surprisingly competent and effective, if tactically naive.

General Mustafa Tlass noted of the new Syrian Army that 'In 1967 we were predominantly an Infantry army, so we had to change quickly, and by 1973 we were an armored one' (quoted in Wakebridge 1976: 28). The costs inherent in such a quick evolution were to be found in the relative paucity of attention paid to the role of the infantry in such an armoured force, as well as a reliance upon the basic level of understanding as far as the new tactics were concerned. Effective combined-arms manoeuvres or assaults were usually beyond the capabilities of the Syrians, and they made particularly poor use of infantry in support of tanks despite having significant numbers of APCs in service. In most cases the infantry, following the Soviet dogma of the time, rarely dismounted from their carriers, and when they did their tactics – little

to no use of manoeuvre or of the terrain, and charging line abreast at entrenched positions – strongly echoed the simple mantras that guided the Red Army of World War II.

Soviet doctrine and tactics were taught, though with varying levels of success as the Soviets found that they often had to deal with unwilling students who did not trust the motives or expertise of their advisors. That being said, some tactical skills, such as night-fighting, certainly did develop, and would prove a most unwelcome surprise for the Israelis. Avigdor Kahalani, a battalion commander on the Golan, was on the receiving end of such new tactics and equipment:

> I wasn't surprised when the Syrians attacked us, and I wasn't surprised with the tactics they used. What did surprise me was the fact that they continued to attack at night. They had the ability to continue their attack at night, and they did it very well. We could not stop them because they skilfully used their infrared lights. This caused us a problem because, whenever we used our infrared Starlight scopes, they were able to detect us and fire on us. It was very frustrating for us because we could see them with infrared binoculars, but we could not stop them. (Quoted in Prosch 1979: 5)

Once the plan of invasion scheduled for 1973 began to take shape, mission-oriented training was undertaken with great seriousness, reflecting to a degree the meticulousness of the planning. Large-scale practice manoeuvres were undertaken and repeated time and again, so every unit understood its role and objectives. In 1973 it would come as an unpleasant shock to the Israelis that 'the relatively convenient enemies of the past, who, time and again, had demonstrated a lack of sophistication, imagination, boldness, and cohesion, became much more sophisticated, both operationally and technologically' (Kober 2011: 178).

Syrian artillery pieces captured as part of the Israeli advance into Syria during the Six-Day War, June 1967. Those on display are examples of the Soviet-made 130mm M-46 towed field gun, recognizable in part due to its long barrel (the gun is 11.73m long) and its rather distinctive 'pepperpot' muzzle brake. Each gun would have a crew of eight and could fire around half-a-dozen 33kg high-explosive shells every minute, up to a maximum range of 27km. With such a range the M-46 could traverse the entire Golan Heights (25km at their widest point) without leaving Syrian soil. It was a fearsomely good piece of artillery and is still in use with the Syrian Army today. (Photo by Stefan Tyszko/Getty Images)

Tel Faher

9 June 1967

BACKGROUND TO BATTLE

During the years leading up to 1967, relations between Israel and the Arab world – and Syria in particular – had been fractious and under near-constant strain. Long-running grievances from the 1948–49 and 1956 wars were exacerbated by fights over water resources and a series of low-intensity military

An Israeli soldier poses atop the hull of a Syrian T-34 medium tank in 1967; the tank lies inverted in a gully after sliding 200m down a cliff-face, coming to rest in one of the tributaries of the River Jordan near the Nahal settlement. (IGPO)

A wrecked Syrian gun emplacement in its fortified position at 'Tawfik' dominating the Tel Katzir Kibbutz and the settlements on the Sea of Galilee. Prior to the Israeli seizure of the Golan Heights in 1967 the Syrians had several fortified positions along the western edge of the Golan allowing them to shell Israeli settlements, either in a deliberate attempt to provoke a reaction from the enemy below, or in retaliation to the latest Israeli raid or incursion. The artillery emplacements were often little more than rather lackadaisical ad hoc turret fortifications made from obsolete, static tanks (such as the PzKpfw IV medium tank shown here), their hulls either buried or positioned hull-down, but their proximity to and occasional shelling of the Jewish settlements was a potent reminder to the Israelis of just how exposed and vulnerable their north-eastern frontier was. (IGPO)

provocations and retaliations from both sides, increasing in regularity and seriousness along the Israeli–Syrian border throughout the first half of 1967. Israel faced a blockade of the Straits of Tiran that threatened both its economy and security. Prior to the outbreak of war the assumption of most observers was of a probable Israeli defeat, with the Arabs themselves certain that the speed and destructiveness of any conflict would be theirs to impose, Colonel Mustafa Tlass of the Syrian Army stating that 'If hostilities break out, the UAR [Egypt] and Syria can destroy Israel in four days at most' (quoted in Dunstan 2009: 22).

Israel's launch of its famed pre-emptive strike on 5 June may have been a strategic masterstroke, but, though long in the planning, the decision to initiate it was born out of a period of intense political stress, as well as an acknowledgement that it was a gamble that could go very wrong. With too many enemies to fight on too many fronts, hitting first was the least worst option available to the Israelis, with Major General Yitzhak Rabin (IDF Chief of Staff 1964–67) stating 'We have to admit the truth. First we'll strike Egypt, and then we'll fight Syria and Jordan as well' (quoted in Oren 2002: 87).

The initial assault on the Egyptian Air Force was immediately devastating, giving the Israel Air Force (IAF) air superiority within hours of the war beginning. The Egyptian ground forces then found themselves on the receiving end of an armoured assault that they simply could not stop. As soon as the war with Egypt was under way the Jordanians moved to the attack by shelling the West Bank, causing the IDF's Central Command to engage on that front; but to the Israelis it must have seemed almost too good to be true that while they were engaged in the centre and the south, no major attack came from the Golan, the Syrians contenting themselves with minor incursions and harassing artillery bombardments. Egypt was the primary focus of the Israeli offensive, and though contingency plans for dealing with both Jordan and Syria existed, the decision as to how – or even whether – to engage them was dependent on the situation as it played out on the ground, rather than as a part of any overarching strategy.

Israeli M51 Sherman medium tanks (nicknamed 'Ishermans' for 'Israeli Shermans') advance through the grim terrain of the Golan. The 12th 'Barak' ('Lightning') Battalion was supported by a force of nine M50 Shermans on their mission to seize the Syrian strongpoints on the Golan, including Tel Faher, where the tanks were picked off one by one, to be followed by the battalion's 19 half-tracks. Overall the Golan proved a challenging environment for Israeli tankers, who found themselves facing T-34-85s, T-54s and old PzKpfw IVs, as well as a range of anti-tank artillery in well-defended emplacements. The Israelis lost around 160 vehicles – about one-third of those they had committed – in this brief campaign, more than in the Sinai and West Bank campaigns combined. (IGPO)

The rapid collapse of Egypt, with the fall of the West Bank and capture of Jerusalem hard on its heels, created an opportunity for the Israelis as far as the Golan was concerned; though plans existed to strike as far as Damascus, a militarily more modest (if politically more realistic) option known as Operation *Hammer* – the capture of the Golan Heights – was the preferred choice. At 0600hrs on 9 June, Brigadier General David Elazar, the officer in charge of Northern Command, was woken by a call from Minister of Defence Moshe Dayan: "'Can you attack?" Dayan asked. However dazed, Elazar replied unhesitatingly. "I can – and right now." "Then attack"' (quoted in Oren 2002: 279).

The Syrian Army, with eight brigades – four in the first line, each reinforced by a battalion of T-34-85 medium tanks or SU-100 tank destroyers, with four more in the second and third lines – plus 265 artillery pieces and more than 200 anti-aircraft guns set along the commanding 300m escarpment of the Golan, was defending barely 60km of front (including Lake Tiberias), and was well prepared for any attack. The area around Tel Faher was the preserve of Colonel Amed Amir's 12th Group Brigade (a group brigade being a Syrian administrative version of a division), consisting of one armoured and three infantry brigades (44th Armoured, 11th Infantry, 132nd and 80th Reserve Infantry). Simon Dunstan notes, however, the serious dearth of properly trained officers:

> With no field experience at all, Ibrahim Isma'il Khahya was appointed as commander of the 8th Infantry Brigade overlooking the vital Bnot Ya'acov Bridge and thought to be one of the most likely avenues of an attack by the IDF. The chief of intelligence on the Golan Heights, Colonel Nash'at Habash was replaced by a lowly captain who happened to be the brother of a high-ranking Ba'ath official. (Dunstan 2009: 25)

The Israeli forces opposing them included Lieutenant Colonel Albert Mendler's 8th Armored Brigade, fresh from the Sinai (with two more armoured brigades, the 37th and 45th, redeploying from the West Bank), and three infantry brigades: the 2nd by Lake Tiberias, the 3rd on the approaches to the Bnot Ya'acov Bridge in the centre of the line, and the 1st – the Golani Brigade – at the northern end of the Hula valley opposite Banias. The Golani Brigade, founded on 28 February 1948, had been something of a second-line outfit in the 1950s, but it had worked hard to become a more professional fighting force. Though its reputation had improved in the years prior to the 1967 war, there was still a degree of prejudice about the Golani and its capabilities, because 'The Golani troops came from the poorest segment of Israeli society and a majority were high school drop-outs, the children of Jews from North Africa and the Middle East. Many Israelis had long feared that the young men of the "Second Israel" would not stand up to the test of battle' (Luttwak & Horowitz 1975: 277).

The Golani Brigade, commanded by Major General Yona Efrat, received its orders from Elazar: 'An infantry force of the Golani Brigade, reinforced by tanks, will capture the fortified positions of Tel-Azaziyat, Tel-Fachr, Burj-Babil, and later the villages of Banyas and Tel-Hamrah' (quoted in Hashavia 1969: 303–04). The 51st 'HaBok'im HaRishon' ('First Breachers') Battalion, led by Lieutenant Colonel Benjamin Inbar, would take Tel Azaziat, while the 12th 'Barak' ('Lightning') Battalion under Lieutenant Colonel Moses 'Musa' Klein, would seize Tel Faher (in Hebrew the name translates as 'The Hill of Glory'). Both battalions were mechanized (mostly the ubiquitous M3 half-track), and would be supported by a company of M50 Sherman medium tanks (nicknamed 'Ishermans': 'Israeli Shermans') drawn from the 8th Armored Brigade to be shared between both battalions, as well as detachments of M3s converted to carry mortars. The 13th 'Gideon' Battalion would remain in reserve, ready to exploit the expected success of the attack and conquer the Banias region.

Infantry from the Golani Brigade in Banias village, 10 June 1967. One of the much sought-after objectives of the Israelis was the area known as the Banias in the northern Golan, which included Banias village at the foot of Mount Hermon, as well as a spring that serves as one of the main sources of the River Jordan. The issue of water was a fraught one throughout the 1950s and especially in the run-up to the 1967 war. Israeli irrigation plans caused friction with the Syrians and Lebanese, who in turn attempted to divert the Banias River from Israeli territory more or less entirely with a series of canals; a scheme that was thwarted by Israeli attacks, including airstrikes. The potentially precarious nature of Israel's water supply had been shown all too clearly, however, and would prove to be one of the motivating factors for Israel's pre-emptive attacks. (IGPO)

MAP KEY

1 **1100hrs:** The 8th Armored Brigade battlegroup moves out and by 1130hrs crosses into the Golan, followed at 1346hrs by the Golani Brigade's 12th 'Barak' ('Lightning') Battalion battlegroup, and at 1454hrs by the 51st 'HaBok'im HaRishon' ('First Breachers') Battalion battlegroup.

2 **c.1500hrs:** The advancing Israelis, mistaking their angle of approach, come under accurate artillery fire from the Syrian defenders of Tel Faher.

3 **c.1530hrs:** Abandoning the flanking manoeuvre, the 12th Battalion commander, Lieutenant Colonel Moses 'Musa' Klein, orders a frontal assault. Lieutenant Aharon Verdi attacks the eastern approaches with 11 men while 12 men under Captain Alex Krinsky attack the northern redoubt; both groups take heavy casualties and are pinned down.

4 **c.1600hrs:** Having lost radio contact with his men, Klein follows Krinsky's angle of approach into the northern objective, but is killed by enemy fire before he can reorganize the attack.

5 **c.1600hrs–c.1730hrs:** Independent groups of Golani soldiers keep up the pressure on the defenders, followed by an organized assault led by Major Zohar Noi that tries to outflank the position to the north.

6 **c.1645hrs:** Captain Avraham Solovitz arrives with six men, fresh from taking Burj Babil. His force penetrates the northern objective, where nearly all of them are killed.

7 **c.1800hrs:** Sayeret Golani scouts, led by Captain Ruben 'Ruvke' Elias, enter the Syrian defences from the east. They advance on the northernmost part of the complex and take it after fierce hand-to-hand fighting.

Battlefield environment

An attack on the Golan Heights was a daunting prospect. The escarpment rose 300m above the plains of Israel, with little in the way of natural cover to mask an approach. The Israelis had marked the Syrian positions and, for the assault by the 8th Armored Brigade and the Golani battalions, had decided on an axis of attack that led up through some of the roughest terrain on a 1:8 incline in the belief that, as it was such a difficult route to use for an attack, it would in consequence be more lightly guarded. Every twist and turn of the route had been reconnoitred and meticulously plotted as Operation *Hammer*, the codename for the attack, was envisaged as a night-time action. The political realities of the war, however, necessitated that the operation be launched in the bright light of day; added to this, the Syrian defences, even though their locations were known and had been targeted for airstrikes and artillery bombardment, were extremely strong. The Golani Brigade's intelligence officer described the defences of Tel Faher: 'The area is mountainous, rocky, full of canyons and difficult for manoeuvring either by vehicle or on foot. The position … comprises gun positions, bunkers, deep and wide communications trenches and numerous tall and seemingly impregnable double-sloped fences, the distance between them being between 5 and 8 meters. The spaces between the fences are mined and filled with spider-webbed fences. Tel-Fachr houses a reinforced company which has part of the battalion supporting weapons including mortars, anti-tank guns and tanks … Every fortified position is protected by its neighbors in the defensive complex and, in turn, protects them' (Quoted in Hashavia 1969: 331–32).

This picture shows Tel Faher, as seen from the approach to the west. The ground was rough and rocky, like much of the Golan, though there was a fair amount of undergrowth as well as trees on the crest of the hill, obscuring many of the enemy bunkers. The Syrians had made the most of the natural defences of Tel Faher, with the site shielded by wire entanglements, bunkers, trenches and fortified gun emplacements. Tel Faher was shaped like a shallow horseshoe, with the main Syrian strongpoints built on the north-western and south-eastern crests of the hill (the left and right 'edges' of the horseshoe), and connected to one another by trenches. The north-western hill was the highest point of Tel Faher, and the most heavily defended. In addition to the tank guns dug in on the hill the Syrians had a battery of 82mm mortars, a pair of recoilless rifles (probably old Soviet 82mm B-10 models) and several heavy machine guns. (CC BY-SA 3.0/Jakednb)

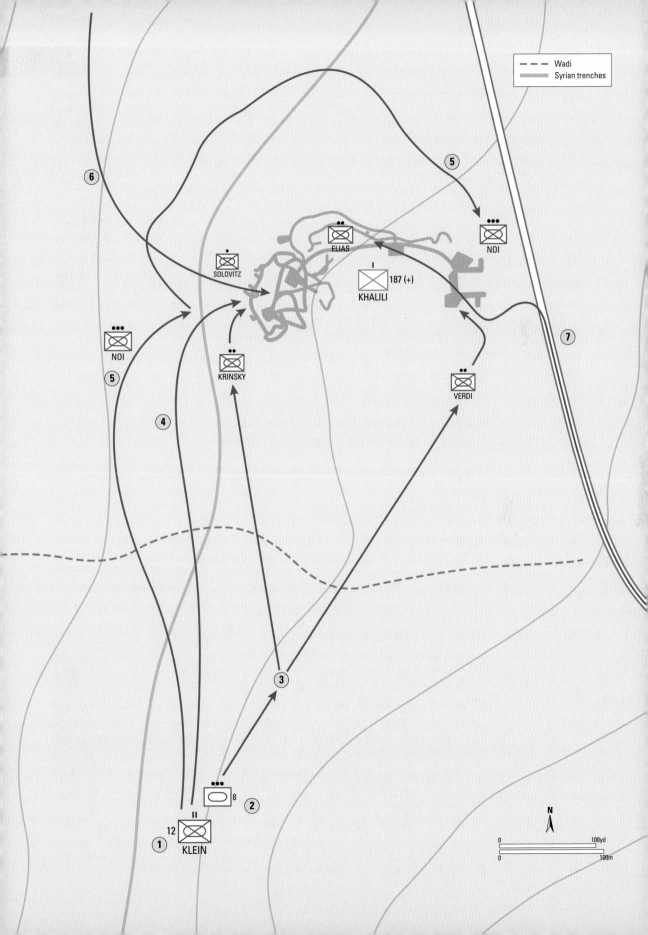

Wadi

Syrian trenches

⑤

⑥

ELIAS ••

SOLOVITZ •

NOI •••

I
KHALILI ⊠ 187 (+)

NOI •••

⑤

KRINSKY ••

VERDI ••

⑦

④

③

••• 8
②

12 II
① ⊠
KLEIN

N

0   100yd
0   100m

INTO COMBAT

The 8th Armored Brigade began to move out at 1100hrs, and as soon as the
Israelis began to pass Giv'at Ha'Em the Syrian artillery started up. Despite
counter-battery fire and airstrikes, the advance continued beneath a near-
constant artillery barrage. By 1130hrs the 8th Armored Brigade crossed the
'Green Line' (the border between Israel and Syria) and began its ascent up the
Golan; when it reached the plateau the brigade would wheel to the right and
make for Qala, with the Golani battlegroups following on and turning to the
left to make for Tel Faher, Tel Azaziat and the Banias beyond.

The Golani battlegroup started out two hours later, crossing the 'Green
Line' at 1346hrs. Efrat's plan of attack was to advance on the Syrian positions
from the west, taking Tel Faher first as it protected Tel Azaziat's rear approaches,
it being assumed that Tel Azaziat would be the more difficult of the two to
storm. Both Tel Azaziat and Tel Faher were each garrisoned by a company
from the Syrian 11th Infantry Brigade, each company having been reinforced
with a pair of PzKpfw IV tank emplacements, while the smaller fortified
positions of Bahriat and Harb a-Suda each had a platoon with two T-34 tanks.
The battlegroup, with its company of Ishermans at the front and the infantry
following behind in half-tracks, would move into the battle zone, the first
tank platoon breaking off to neutralize the T-34s at Bahriat, the remaining
tank platoons leading the 12th Battalion to Tel Faher; the 51st Battalion
would follow behind, mopping-up Bahriat and moving into position to
assault Tel Azaziat, which they would take as soon as the 12th Battalion had
stormed Tel Faher and moved on to Burj Babil.

As the Golani columns advanced, it quickly became clear that the initial
efforts to reduce Tel Faher were running into difficulties, so Efrat switched
priorities: instead of the 12th Battalion taking Tel Faher and offering support to
the 51st Battalion, the latter force would proceed at once to Tel Azaziat, storm
it, and then offer support to the 12th Battalion at Tel Faher. The 51st Battalion's
attack on Tel Azaziat, the more feared of the two objectives, ran like clockwork;
the Israeli armour feinted to the west, drawing the garrison's fire, while Inbar's
column of half-tracks crept around the rear, with five of them reaching the
summit, the commander's own vehicle in the vanguard. Dismounting from
their vehicles, the Golani soldiers immediately went into trench clearing, a task
for which they had trained repeatedly in the preceding days and weeks.

For Tel Faher, though, the plan seemed to go wrong almost at once. The
12th Battalion's supposed advance around the rear of objective never happened,
as the rough terrain obscured the flanking path it was supposed to take, leading
the Israelis to approach the Syrian fortifications more or less head-on.
Advancing towards the hill, the column found itself under accurate and intense
artillery fire that immediately started to take its toll on men and vehicles. Three
tanks and four half-tracks were hit in quick succession, one exploding,
mortarman Israel Huberman recalling: 'There was an ocean of flames. I
suddenly felt very hot. I was burning up, I caught fire' (quoted in Segev 2007:
473). His clothes ablaze, Huberman was tackled to the ground by an officer
who managed to put out the flames that had engulfed him, saving his life.

For the Syrians, as noted in their official report of the action, the advance
of the Israelis caused a degree of confusion and panic, with lapses in command
exacerbating the stress of combat:

With the enemy just 700 meters away, under heavy shelling, the platoon in the front trench prepared for battle. The platoon commander sent Private Jalil 'Issa to the company commander to request permission to take cover, but 'Issa could not find him. The platoon commander sent another runner who returned with Private Fajjar Hamdu Karnazi who reported on the company commander's disappearance. When the enemy reached 600 meters, Sgt. Muhammad Yusuf Ibrahim fired a 10-inch anti-tank gun [probably not a '10 inch' gun as there was nothing of that calibre there, but likely a B-10 recoilless rifle] and knocked out the lead tank. But then he and his squad commander were killed. The enemy column advanced. First Sergeant Anwar Barbar, in charge of the second 10-inch gun, could not be found. The platoon commander searched for him but unsuccessfully ... Private Hajj al-Din, who was killed just minutes later, took the gun and fired it alone, knocking out two tanks and forcing the column to retreat. But when the platoon commander tried to radio the information to headquarters, nobody answered. (Quoted in Oren 2002: 283)

Realizing the damage the Syrian guns were doing, 'Musa' Klein abandoned the flanking manoeuvre and opted for a direct attack instead, despite the fact that the brigade intelligence officer had noted that 'a frontal, direct attack is doomed to failure' (quoted in Hashavia 1969: 332). Having first detailed a company under Captain Avraham Solovitz to take Burj Babil, about 1km away, which was acting as an outer defence of Tel Faher, Klein then ordered the battalion's A Company, under Lieutenant Aharon Verdi, to storm Tel Faher. Progress was slow under the fire of the Syrian guns, with three of the company's half-tracks knocked out and a fourth damaged with more than

500m still to go. Verdi gathered his small force – 25 men in all – and continued the advance on foot. Despite the Israelis' low numbers Verdi decided to split his force, sending a dozen men with Captain Alex Krinsky to assault the main position on the north-western hill, while he attacked the south-eastern end of the Syrian defensive line.

Captain Ahmad Ibrahim Khalili, commanding a company of the 187th Infantry Battalion that held Tel Faher, watched as the Israelis approached his lines at the best possible place: 'It was one of our most fortified positions … It placed them directly in our crosshairs' (quoted in Oren 2002: 283). Verdi and his small force struggled up the rough ground, fighting their way through the fences with two soldiers, David Shirazi and Ya'acov Hutzira, throwing themselves onto the barbed-wire entanglements to act as human bridges for the rest of the men to get across; they made it into the Syrian line through a bunker that had been knocked out by a tank shell. The small force immediately began clearing bunker after bunker, using phosphorus grenades to force the Syrians out into the open where they were shot down. Nevertheless, the advance took its toll on the small force, Private Shlomo Ben-Bassat describing how

> I ran to the left with Kalman, my NCO. We ran through the trenches, clearing out bunkers, until suddenly we saw an alcove with beds and boxes in it. Kalman told me, 'I'll go in and you wait outside.' But no sooner had he entered [the alcove] when he was hit by burst of fire from a wounded Syrian inside. Kalman managed to stumble out – he fell and died. Then the Syrian came out. He saw me and immediately started pleading to me for his life. He stood there with his gun still smoking from the bullets that killed Kalman. I avenged his blood. (Quoted in Oren 2002: 283)

Verdi's unit pushed onward, attacking an anti-tank gun emplacement along the way, until the south-eastern bunkers and trenches were finally cleared; but the cost was high: ammunition was running out, medical supplies were exhausted, and most of the men had taken multiple wounds (Verdi himself had been hit by a shell splinter at the beginning of the attack). The small group of Israelis, too weak to advance but with too many wounded to retreat, was pinned by fire from the larger north-western hill.

The 12 men under Captain Krinsky who had broken away to attack the north-eastern flank of Tel Faher had made it up the side of the hill, scrambling over wire fences. They fought their way into a part of the bunker complex with a boldness that seemed to catch the Syrians off-guard, but at significant cost in dead (including Krinsky himself) and wounded, with only two men, one of them Corporal Yitzhak Hamaway, unhurt:

> In the center of the objective only I myself and another soldier remained untouched and the Syrians did not stop sniping at us. About ten minutes later, the fit soldier went down to call for help … I attempted to establish contact by means of my communications set, in vain. And my ammunition was running out. I had only two magazines left, and one of them was half empty. (Quoted in Hashavia 1969: 354)

At the foot of the hill Klein was effectively blind; the command half-track – and with it communications to brigade headquarters – had been knocked out in the initial advance, and he couldn't raise the small force he had sent into

Tel Faher on the radio. In the Israeli fashion he decided to assess the situation for himself, and so with his communications officer Lieutenant Moshe Harel he made his way up the northern flank of the hill, following Krinksy's path. Hamaway was overjoyed to see his commander appear on the scene, and joined Klein and Harel as Klein pushed forward into the trench system:

> We ran, Musa [Klein] and I, through the trenches … Whenever a helmet popped up, we couldn't tell if it was one of ours or not. Suddenly in front of us stood a soldier whom we couldn't identify. The battalion commander shouted the password and when the soldier didn't answer, he fired a burst at him but missed. We jumped out of the trench, ran five meters, and then Musa fell on his face … killed by the Syrian soldier he'd missed. Our radio man [Harel] waited for him to leap up again, then shot him. (Quoted in Oren 2002: 284)

With his commander dead and Syrian resistance still fierce, Harel left the hill to contact Brigade HQ, letting them know what was happening. In response Elazar despatched Major Zohar Noi to take command and reorganize the offensive.

In the interim, small bands of Golani soldiers, on their own initiative, continued to make their way up the slopes and to press home the attack; a half-track carrying nine men made its way around the rear of the hill, coming to a halt near Verdi's position only to be hit almost immediately by a rocket-propelled grenade (RPG), killing five and injuring two, with one of the two unhurt survivors wounded within minutes of getting to the lieutenant's position. Verdi himself had finally been able to get through to Brigade HQ on the radio and had been told to hold on, reinforcements were on their way. In reality, as there were only three 'whole ones' in his position, holding on – and hoping the Syrians didn't launch a counter-attack – was all he could do;

The rusted remains of an M3 half-track on the road between Tel Azaziat and Tel Faher, lying where it was destroyed during the Golani advance, 9 June 1967. Moving up difficult terrain while under anti-tank and artillery fire from well dug-in, determined defenders was a harrowing experience, especially in the venerable open-topped M3, as noted by one soldier who took part, Haim Brom: 'It was a horrifying ascent … There was a smell of burning, and not just of things. The sense was that it was people too, the smell of people … Anyway, it was something I had never smelled. The people who came later didn't notice it, maybe they just saw the scorched halftracks, but that smell, it gets into your brain. We saw the bodies of our own guys … it was a brutal battle' (quoted in Segev 2007: 425). (CC BY-SA 3.0/ Jakednb)

Trench fighting at Tel Faher

The scene shows a dramatic close-quarters fight between Golani soldiers of the 12th Battalion and elements from the Syrian 187th Infantry Battalion in the trench complex on Tel Faher, 9 June 1967. The attack on Tel Faher was supposed to be quick and easy, a precursor to the seizure of Tel Azaziat which was thought of as a more difficult nut to crack. The initial Israeli plan to outflank the position fell apart almost immediately, leading the commander of the 12th Battalion, Lieutenant Colonel Moses 'Musa' Klein, to gamble on a frontal assault instead. Losing men and most of their vehicles on the way, the Israelis nevertheless penetrated the Syrian stronghold in two places, and for the next few hours small groups of Golani soldiers, sometimes numbering no more than half a dozen, would fight their way in, often on their own initiative, to battle with the entrenched Syrians. As the illustration shows, the fighting could be conducted at very close quarters, eventually degenerating into hand-to-hand combat towards

the end of the battle. Israelis would try to clear bunkers and trenches with hand grenades and bursts of fire from Uzi submachine guns, and the Syrians in turn would ambush their attackers from well-concealed firing positions, or pick them off with sniper fire. Casualties on both sides were high, with the majority of Israelis on Tel Faher being killed or wounded during their attempts to clear the Syrians from the bunkers and trenches that criss-crossed the top of the hill. Syrian resistance only broke when the majority of the defenders were wounded or dead; few prisoners were taken. The general collapse of the entire Syrian front line the day after the battle of Tel Faher gave the impression that the whole Syrian campaign had been a walkover from start to finish, but for the Israelis who fought their way up on to the Golan, and who had to wrest places like Tel Faher from their stubborn defenders, the story was far more complicated than that.

that, and reassure his wounded men that 'in a little while, in a little while, the boys will be here to evacuate you' (quoted in Hashavia 1969: 367).

Zohar Noi arrived at the site of the battle and quickly organized an attack on the north-western position following Krinsky's line of approach, but the endeavour was fiercely beaten back at the cost of both dead and wounded. Pulling back, Noi's men then piled into five half-tracks and made their way around the rear of Tel Faher, taking mortar and gunfire (which wounded Noi in the neck) as they went. Fortunately, the Syrian mortars proved mostly inaccurate and the force dismounted and moved into the cleared and abandoned Syrian trenches in the centre of the position, from where they provided supporting fire for another Israeli group who were advancing across the north-western hill. That group was a small force of six men under Solovitz; fresh from their capture of Burj Babil, they had arrived at the north-western position. Following Krinsky's route, they were able to penetrate into the complex where Noi's men had been rebuffed. The fire support that he was receiving from Noi's force didn't help Solovitz, however:

> There was a trench which looked very innocent but which concealed what was actually a manned bunker. When 'Solo' jumped into the trench and started running along it, he was shot in the back and fell on his face. Four of his men jumped into the trench after him and every one of them met with a similar fate. Only the last of the group noticed what was happening, thrust a hand grenade into the bunker, and avenged the blood of his comrades. (Hashavia 1969: 370)

Though the fighting had been hard and unforgiving, the Syrian position had been much-weakened by terrible casualties that left the majority of the defenders wounded or dead. Around this time a small group of Sayeret Golani scouts under Captain Ruben 'Ruvke' Elias, who had been wounded twice already, arrived. As the situation at Tel Faher worsened, Efrat had pulled the

Syrian soldiers walking into captivity as Israeli tanks pass them by, 11 June 1967. There were many theories as to why the Arab armies had collapsed in such short order, though Michael Hadow – the British ambassador to Israel, 1965–69 – 'stressed the personal element, the stark disparity between the Israeli and the Arab soldier: "These were not elite professional troops lavishly equipped with the most modern equipment, but for the most part civilian reservists, with comparatively limited training behind them, who were carried into battle in civilian transport, and were supplied and supported by essentially civilian services. By comparison, the professional Arab armies showed a total lack of appreciation of the essential elements of modern warfare, and an almost equal inability to use the sophisticated weapons and equipment provided by their Russian quartermasters. Their leadership on almost all fronts was inept to a degree which hardly seems possible after 10 years of preparation and training for a war which was to bring about Israel's annihilation"' (quoted in Oren 2002: 311). (IGPO)

scouts from their assigned task of protecting the Golani Brigade's troop transports and ordered them to approach Tel Faher from the rear and add their weight to the attacks on the beleaguered Syrians. Entering from the east, they made contact with Verdi's men while a squad broke off and advanced on the northern objective, probing their way through trenches and bunkers. The fighting degenerated into a series of intimately vicious hand-to-hand encounters, with men wrestling and clubbing their way through the few remaining Syrian positions, as Elias experienced when his Uzi submachine gun ran out of ammunition at the very moment he confronted a 'broad-shouldered' Syrian officer:

['Ruvke' Elias] attacked the Syrian empty-handed. The Syrian tried to fire his carbine, but apparently something went wrong with his gun too. He pulled out his pistol from its holster on his hip. Ruvke's fist hit him so hard that his own shoulder was dislocated. The Syrian started pounding his revolver on Ruvke's head. The latter hugged him with all his might with his good arm and his aching one alike, and started to roll him all over the trench. Ruvke succeeded in wresting away the Syrian's gun, but the struggle was still bitter. Muki, a member of the patrol who had jumped into the tunnel after Ruvke ... didn't know how to save him. A shot might hit the patrol commander instead of the Syrian officer. Muki, broad-shouldered and muscular, put his arm around the Syrian's neck, kicked him in his feet, and tried to loosen his hold on Ruvke. In vain. The Syrian was fighting desperately. Just then Captain David [Cohen] jumped into the trench – a jump that cost him a broken ankle. He kicked the Syrian and pushed him to the wall of the trench. There the Syrian was killed with a short burst. (Hashavia 1969: 374–75)

القنيطرة

Quneitra

A small group of Israelis posing in a captured Syrian GAZ-69 light truck by a sign to Kuneitra on the Golan Heights. The capture of Kuneitra on the last day of the Six-Day War was an important element of the overall Israeli push to secure the Golan, and the town would become a prominent strategic feature in the Yom Kippur War six years later, being fought over and captured by both sides on several occasions. In Israeli hands at the time of the Yom Kippur War ceasefire, Kuneitra was due to be handed back to the Syrians as part of the peace agreement, but incensed Israeli settlers stripped the town of anything of value and razed the rest to the ground. It was never rebuilt by the Syrians, and remains as a lingering testament to the bad blood that dominated – and to a significant degree still dominates – Israeli–Syrian relations. (IGPO)

The Golani scouts broke the last of the Syrian resistance, with Tel Faher finally falling at about 1800hrs. Elazar observed that 'at the post and in the trenches there were at least sixty bodies spread about. There was hand-to-hand fighting there, fighting with fists, knives, teeth and rifle butts' (quoted in Bowen 2004: 278). Efrat gave due praise to his enemy: 'The Syrians neither fled nor surrendered ... They stopped fighting when they were dead' (quoted in Hashavia 1969: 335). Of the fort's defenders only one officer and two men had surrendered; 26 more were captured and 62 lay dead, with only a small group of eight men under Corporal Mustafa Suliman managing to slip away. The Israelis lost 31 killed and 82 wounded in the battle; the victory was hard-won, with Efrat saying:

> I don't know whether in the entire history of the IDF many battles such as this one were fought ... At Tel Fachr there were dozens of casualties, not in one short salvo but in three hours' fighting, and not out of the sight of their comrades-in-arms, but right in front of their eyes, in the trenches! Never will it be said that the Golani Brigade is just another infantry unit! (Quoted in Hashavia 1969: 358)

Outpost 107

6–10 October 1973

BACKGROUND TO BATTLE

The battles fought by the IDF on 9 June 1967 to break through the first Syrian line on the Golan were hard-won. As morning broke on 10 June the Israelis braced themselves for the inevitable counter-attack; instead, the whole Syrian Army seemed to crumble away in front of them. The commander of the 8th Infantry Brigade, Ibrahim Isma'il Khahya, remembered: 'We received orders to block the roads leading to Quneitra. But

Israeli armour attacking the Syrian line on the Golan Heights. Command and control of the armoured units would prove to be critical in stopping the Syrian advance. Lieutenant Colonel Avigdor Kahalani, commander of the 77th Armored Battalion during the Yom Kippur War, describes how to lead in such a situation in terms that many Israeli commanders, whatever branch they might be in, would find familiar: 'In a battalion-sized unit, most of the time you are talking to your companies on the radio. It is very important for you, the commander, to give to your units the feeling you are with them all of the time. You must control them from the front. They must see you up there with them. You cannot control from behind them. Every commander must lead by personal example. Sometimes the soldiers are very young and afraid. But they will follow the leader who is with them. However, they need the leaders between them and the enemy. The leaders should be up front' (quoted in Prosch 1979: 9). (IGPO)

Israeli M51 Sherman tanks form up for a counter-attack against Syrian armour, 8 October 1973. The M51 was a typical Israeli hybrid made up from an M4A4 Sherman with a strengthened suspension and chassis, and which was armed with a cut-down version of the French-made 105mm CN105-F1 rifled tank gun originally developed for the AMX-30 light tank. Note the projection at the rear of the turret, this being a counterweight required to balance out the load of the gun. The Israelis, with internal lines of communication and a defensive posture prepared around well-constructed tank positions, were better situated than the Syrians, but the landscape of the Golan would ensure that the armoured warfare conducted there would be of a very different nature to that witnessed in the fast-moving expanses of the Sinai. (IGPO)

then the fall of the city was announced and that caused many of my soldiers to leave the front and run back to Syria while those roads were still open. They piled onto vehicles. It further crushed our morale. I retreated before I ever saw an enemy soldier' (quoted in Oren 2002: 301). The Israelis couldn't catch up with their retreating enemy, they were falling back so fast.

Studious rebuilding of every aspect of the armed forces was needed and, with the coming to power of Hafez al-Assad in 1970, Syria had at last the political stability to see such a programme through. Great use was made of Soviet advisers, planners, and technicians as the Syrian Army was reborn as a more or less wholly Soviet-armed and -trained entity, vastly better equipped and more powerful than it had been in 1967. Such a force had one primary military objective: 'the defeat of the Israeli armed forces deployed [on] the Syrian plateau and seizure of strategic land areas which would pave the way for the complete liberation of the occupied territories in order to impose a just and peaceful solution to the problem' (el Badri et al. 1978: 16–17). The Israelis had assumed it would take two generations for the Arab states to recover from the enormity of their loss, and yet for Syria, in concert with President Anwar Sadat's newly revitalized Egypt, the prospect of seizing the victory the Arab world so badly desired was now within arm's reach a scant six years after the embarrassments of 1967.

In contrast to the Syrians, for the Israelis a certain 'complacency to the point of hubris' (Kober 2011: 177) had settled on the country in general and the IDF in particular. Martin van Creveld observed that the IDF's swollen sense of its own accomplishments led it to drag its heels on establishing new formations, and to not properly support those it already had: 'Of greater immediate significance were decisions such as canceling the purchase of

Israeli troops take cover by the side of the road to avoid Syrian aircraft on a strafing run, 8 October 1973. The Syrian Arab Air Force (SyAAF) in concert with Iraqi forces launched heavy, repeated attacks on Israeli ground targets from the outset of the war. They flew 270 sorties on the first day, mainly with Sukhoi Su-7 and Su-20 fighter-bombers protected by MiG-21s providing a fighter screen to keep the Israeli Mirage IIIs, F-4 Phantoms and A-4 Skyhawks at bay. Although the intensity of Syrian air attacks waned somewhat after the first day, the pilots of the SyAAF continued to harass and attack Israeli positions despite an increasingly deadly Israeli fightback: 'it continued sending MiG-21s on CAPs [Combat Air Patrols] over the front, while others escorted strikes which caused severe losses to Israeli positions. Most packages comprised six to twelve ground-attack aircraft, escorted by four to eight MiG-21s. Except for their top cover, the Syrians flew in such tight formations that Israeli radars could not accurately assess their number. Sometimes such tactics even resulted in Israeli interceptors failing to detect Syrian interceptors' (Nicolle & Cooper 2004: 48). (IGPO)

additional naval vessels, bridging equipment, tank transporters, and APCs; the IDF was so "tankomanic" by this time that it considered the possibility of setting up an armored division without an organic artillery regiment' (Creveld 2002: 219). Indeed the proportion of artillery (the majority of it self-propelled) to tanks was about half what it should have been. The venerable fleet of M3s still dominated the mechanized units, the newer M113 only having replaced around a seventh of the IDF's half-track fleet by the time war came again in 1973. Even then, 'Half-tracks, and APCs, serving both as personnel and weapons carriers, were considered at best secondary vehicles, and often as superfluous impediments in an armoured battle. If, as in 1973, limited road facilities required the setting of movement priorities, tanks, considered as the primary weapons system, were brought forward first and engaged without support' (Rothenberg 1979: 159).

On the Golan the Israeli defences seemed well ordered. A vast anti-tank ditch, 6m wide and 4m deep, ran the length of the border with Syria. From north to south along the Purple Line (the United Nations-mandated 1967 ceasefire zone between Israel and Syria along the Golan, so-called because of its purple colour on UN maps) were 17 strongpoints supported by 112 blockhouses and pillboxes. The approaches to each strongpoint were heavily mined, and each of the outposts was supported to the rear by three tanks on well-sited, specially built firing platforms, with two understrength armoured brigades (the 188th 'Barak' and the 7th, 177 tanks in all) a few kilometres further back. The infantry manning the outposts and bunkers were from the 13th 'Gideon' Battalion of the Golani Brigade. At the rear, 44 guns in 11 batteries provided artillery support. Against this thinly held line the Syrian plan of attack, called *Mashrua* 110 ('Operation 110'), would throw three reinforced infantry divisions (the 5th, 7th and 9th) and two armoured divisions (the 1st and 3rd), with more forces in reserve: around 1,400 tanks, 950 artillery pieces, over 100 surface-to-air missile (SAM) batteries and 70,000 men (28,000 of them mechanized infantry) in all.

MAP KEY

1 1400hrs, 6 October: The Syrian attack begins with a massive artillery bombardment and the advance of the 7th and 9th Infantry divisions.

2 7 October: The Syrian attack continues – first serious armoured and infantry attacks on Outpost 107.

3 8 October: Lieutenant Shmuel Yakhin's small tank force withdraws, leaving Outpost 107 unsupported.

4 9 October: The last Syrian assault is mounted by elements of the 7th and 9th Infantry and 3rd Armoured divisions plus a tank detachment from the Presidential Guard.

5 10 October: In the afternoon an Israeli relief column under the command of Lieutenant Colonel Yair Nafshi arrives at Outpost 107.

Battlefield environment

The area of the Golan that became known as the 'Valley of Tears' was one of the few areas along the Golan Heights that offered a Syrian armoured attack some chance of success because it hosted the passage of the Damascus–Kuneitra–Safed road, and also – unlike the majority of that rough borderland – there was some small amount of room to manoeuvre. Thus it became one of the two axes of the general Syrian attack, the other being the 'Rafid Gap' to the south. To the immediate south of the Damascus road lay the town of Kuneitra, captured from the Syrians in 1967 and now a mostly uninhabited ruin with the exception of an IDF outpost. To the west of the anti-tank ditch lay a shallow valley with several key outcrops of volcanic rock, from south to north: Merom Golan, the position known as 'Booster' to the Israelis, and Hermonit.

Outpost 107, one of the strongpoints built by the Israelis all along the Purple Line (the marker of the UN-mandated 1967 ceasefire zone), was situated a little differently from the others thanks to the area's topography and the particular role the outpost was meant to play. Positioned to watch over the Damascus–Kuneitra road, it lay 500m to the east of the anti-tank ditch, and was on a plain rather than a more-easily defensible rise: 'All the other bunkers along the cease-fire line were fronted by a continuous antitank ditch, stretching from the Hermon, in the North, to the border with Jordan, in the South. Because of the way the land lay around Bunker 107, however, it had been placed in front of the ditch by a considerable distance. The garrison was thus expected to carry on a fight against attacking Syrian forces well in front of and physically isolated from other Israeli forces. If attacked, the soldiers at Bunker 107 would have to man an exposed 360-degree defensive perimeter' (Asher & Hammel 1987: 36–37).

An image of the abandoned bunker at Tel A-Saki on the Golan Heights. Outpost 107 fell on the wrong side of the ceasefire line at the end of the 1973 war and was destroyed by the Syrians in 1974; all the outposts that the Israelis built along the Purple Line were similar in style and design, however, and the position at Tel A-Saki conveys well enough how Outpost 107 would have looked at the time. Outpost 107 was 'generally typical of Israeli positions guarding the cease-fire line. It was well constructed, capable of withstanding heavy artillery fire. Tank or infantry attacks from across no-man's-land would be minimized by a belt of mines planted along the approaches from Syria and in front of a stout barbed-wire barrier. The garrisons had light antitank weapons, chiefly bazookas, but they would also be amply protected against armored attacks by supporting armored units of their own' (Asher & Hammel 1987: 36). The outposts would also have heavy machine guns fixed to pintle mounts set in the concrete of the bunker, with 7.62mm FN MAG general-purpose machine guns and .50-calibre M2HB Browning heavy machine guns both used in such a role. (Courtesy of William Jacobson)

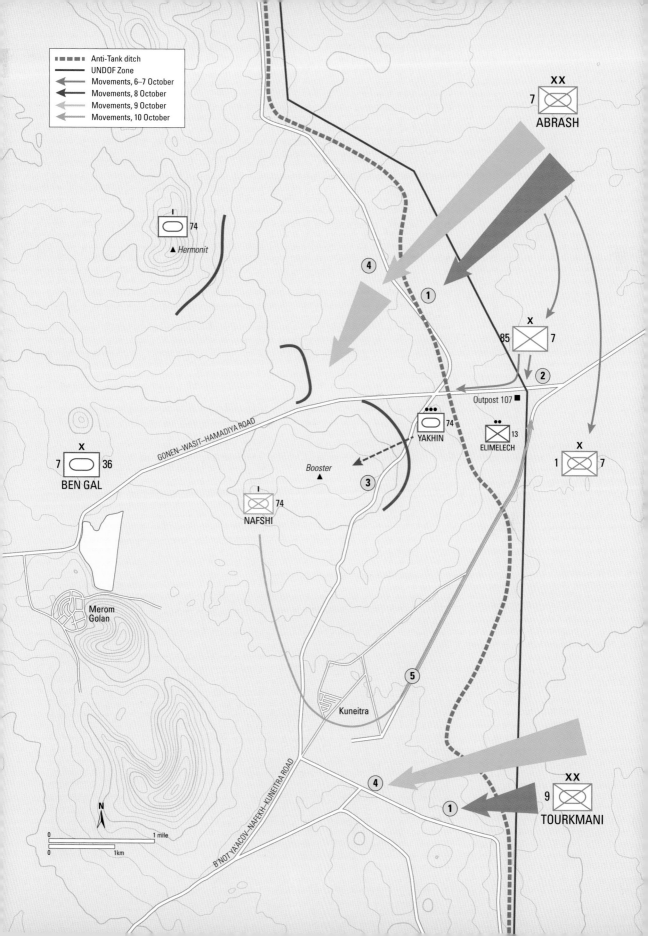

Legend

- - - - - Anti-Tank ditch
———— UNDOF Zone
← Movements, 6–7 October
← Movements, 8 October
← Movements, 9 October
← Movements, 10 October

XX
7 ⊠ ABRASH

I
74 ▲ Hermonit

4

1

X
85 ⊠ 7

2

Outpost 107 ■

X
7 ⬭ 36
BEN GAL

GONEN–WASIT–HAMADIYA ROAD

•••
74 YAKHIN

••
⊠ 13
ELIMELECH

X
1 ⊠ 7

▲ Booster

3

I
74 ⊠ NAFSHI

Merom
Golan

5

Kuneitra

4

1

XX
9 ⊠ TOURKMANI

N

0 _____ 1 mile
0 _____ 1km

B'NOT YA'ACOV–NAFEKH–KUNEITRA ROAD

INTO COMBAT

At the start of the Syrian attack the 7th Infantry Division's 85th Infantry Brigade headed west to the Gonen road while the 1st Mechanized Brigade made for Kuneitra to the south-west. The first Israeli unit they would come across was the small team of men in Outpost 107.

Like most of such outposts up and down the line, Outpost 107 was garrisoned by a small team of men from the Golani Brigade's 13th 'Gideon' Battalion. The commander was Lieutenant Avraham Elimelech, commissioned for just seven months and in charge of his new command for only a matter of weeks. His small garrison of a dozen men had been increased to 19 the morning war began, the extra men being drawn from various posts of the battalion's support company; the garrison was expected to work in concert with the three tanks from the 74th Armored Battalion of the 188th 'Barak' Armored Brigade that constituted their back-up. Such armour was positioned so as to have 'the open, undulating ground fronting the ceasefire line under accurate fire, preregistered in interlocking and mutually supporting bands. Several tank battalions based in camps along the length of the Golan would provide the tanks as needed, and they would also mount spoiling attacks at platoon or company strength, as appropriate' (Asher & Hammel 1987: 36). As the historian Abraham Rabinovich relates:

> In the event of a serious attack, the strongpoint's survival would depend on the tank platoon posted to its rear. In the few weeks he had been at 107, Elimelekh had had intensive sessions with the platoon commander, Lt. Shmuel Yakhin, to work out cooperation in the event of an attack. The two officers identified elements of the topography together so that each would quickly understand what the other was referring to. They agreed that the tanks would deal with Syrian armor and the strongpoint with infantry. The battalion intelligence officer visited Yom Kippur morning and told Elimelekh that the Syrians might attempt to snatch a strongpoint in the coming battle day and take its garrison prisoner. A likely target, said the officer, making a snatching movement with his hand, was Strongpoint 107. (Rabinovich 2004: 97)

An Israeli soldier looks on as an IAF A-4 Skyhawk offers close air support to IDF units advancing on the Golan during the Yom Kippur War. The overwhelming might of the IAF in the Six-Day War of 1967 was the most dramatic feature of that conflict, all but winning the conflict on the first day, but by 1973 the Israelis found themselves operating against a far more dangerous and capable enemy. Though the Arab air forces were generally not a match for Israeli pilots in air-to-air encounters, the wholesale adoption of Soviet SAM defence systems and tactics by both the Egyptians and Syrians bore much fruit. Low-flying sorties of the sort shown here came in below the 'missile net' but were vulnerable to the depredations of ground fire, particularly from the Russian-made, Syrian-operated ZSU-23-4 anti-aircraft system sporting four radar-guided 23mm autocannons; each tank regiment would usually have a battery of four ZSU-23-4s and they would exact a punishing toll on IAF low-level attacks in the early days of the war. On the first day of the air war over the Golan the Israelis lost 30 A-4 Skyhawks and ten F-4 Phantoms to SAM-6 and ZSU-23-4 batteries, compared to 46 aircraft lost throughout the whole of the Six-Day War. (IGPO)

The thunderous artillery barrage, the roar and shudder of hundreds of tank engines and the clouds of dust thrown up by the massive Syrian columns quickly did for such a quaint notion. At 1350hrs, four aircraft passed over the post, from north to south. The lookout called to Elimelech, and in that instant the shelling started. Despite this, Lieutenant Elimelech and his radioman remained outside in a sheltered position, calling the observation points on the hills to their rear to find out how the situation to the front was developing; but the Syrian barrage was encompassing the depth of the whole line, blinding them. When the artillery fire let up 'Elimelekh could see through binoculars a mass of tanks and trucks coming down the Damascus road. Infantrymen aboard the trucks held their rifles in the air and pumped them up and down in exultation' (Rabinovich 2004: 148).

Lieutenant Yakhin's three tanks manoeuvred on to the firing ramps that supported the outpost, opening fire at a range of around 1,800m. The Israeli tank gunners, trained repeatedly to repel enemy armour in such circumstances, wreaked considerable havoc on the advancing Syrians, knocking out some of their tanks well before their own guns came within effective range. Yakhin's small force was temporarily reinforced by a further seven tanks that helped add to the growing carnage along the Damascus road, all the while enjoying a seeming invulnerability as the slow-firing Syrians failed to land a single kill. Rabinovich notes how 'To the Israelis' astonishment, Syrian tanks kept coming, swerving around those which had been hit. It was not until some thirty tanks were knocked out that the column turned south out of range' (Rabinovich 2004: 149). The single-mindedness of the Syrian attack appalled the more tactically minded Israelis such as Avigdor Kahalani, commander of the 77th Armored Battalion: 'If he were leading the attack, he'd have the tanks approach cautiously, darting up the valley from one bit of cover to the next. But the Syrians' strategy was direct, and suicidal: They charged no matter the cost. And they would continue until nothing was left to stop them' (Blum 2004: 194).

The situation on the Golan was critically serious almost from the first moment. Thanks to Syrian bridging units the anti-tank ditch was crossed in several places, with the seemingly unending columns of tanks and APCs forcing breaches in various parts of the line, with the Rafid Gap proving especially vulnerable to the massive weight of the Syrian advance. The casualties that were being inflicted on those Syrian columns were horrendous, and yet they continued on, through the day and into the darkness, where they proved to be well equipped with infrared night-fighting gear.

That night a Syrian battalion of tanks and other vehicles arrived on the road just 300m shy of Outpost 107. Elimelech acted as spotter for

A posed shot of an infantryman with an 82mm IMI M20 Super-Bazooka during summer manoeuvres in the Negev, 1960. The Israeli infantry were not well supplied with anti-armour weapons; a home-grown version of a *Panzerschreck*, the IMI M20 Super-Bazooka was developed in the early 1950s, but domestic production never came close to supplying enough weapons for the IDF, who purchased numbers of 73mm LRAC Mle 1950 anti-tank rocket-launchers from France and later 83mm RL-83 Blindicides from Belgium, among others. Infantry units were often lacking any anti-tank weapons at all, though they were to be found in at least some of the Israeli forward observation bunkers that dotted the front line of the Golan, as used by the redoubtable Private Joseph Zadok in Outpost 107. (IGPO)

The battle for Outpost 107

Israeli view: The small garrison of Outpost 107 fight off an attempted incursion by elements of a Syrian motorized unit. Private Joseph Zadok, the bazookaman of Outpost 107, accounted for six Syrian tanks over the duration of the battle, the first of which he had knocked out just prior to the encounter shown here, and which now burns fiercely. Despite being lightly manned, the Israeli outposts were far from defenceless, with most having four pintle-mounted machine guns. In addition, all the outposts were designed to be supported by the guns of a tank platoon, and could also call on artillery and air support as and when needed. The outposts themselves were well-constructed bunker complexes that could withstand significant and long-term artillery bombardment. They were also ringed with wire fences, with the spaces between the fences dotted with minefields of both anti-personnel and anti-armour variety. The troops inside the bunker were lightly armed, mostly with Uzis, though each outpost was supposed to have at least one bazookaman who would be armed with one of a variety of anti-tank weapons depending on availability.

Syrian view: A Syrian motorized squad has dismounted from their BTR-60PB APC and are attempting to make their way through the wire entanglements when they are caught in a burst of machine-gun fire from the IDF outpost. A T-55 main battle tank which had gone in to the attack in support of the infantry has been hit by an Israeli bazooka round and is now burning fiercely away to the left. The attack shown here was one of a number launched against Outpost 107, and indeed most of the other outposts strung out along the line. The great Syrian columns, often hundreds of vehicles long, would pass within a few hundred metres of Outpost 107, but made no concerted effort to reduce the Israeli fortification despite the fact that the outpost was inflicting casualties on them, either directly through their anti-tank fire, through directing the gunnery of their supporting tank platoon, or in their role as a forward observation post for Israeli artillery and airstrikes. The first wave of a traditional mechanized advance would bypass such an obstacle, happy enough to suppress it and neutralize its effectiveness through bombardment or some other method, leaving the job of mopping up to subsequent waves.

A trio of knocked-out Syrian Army T-54/55 main battle tanks. Despite the apparent high quality of the Syrian tank crews, their horrendous losses were not all down to the extreme capability of Israeli tank gunners to score hits at great distances. At a tactical level, the Syrians were hopelessly outclassed through a mixture of inexperience, insufficient training, and finding themselves in combat against a motivated, highly experienced enemy that treated all aspects of tank warfare with an almost religious zeal: 'Syrian tank units only rarely maneuvered in battle, and on those few occasions when they did, their actions were slow, tentative and predictable ... Because Syrian armor simply surged forward mindlessly, they often created severe traffic jams and "target-rich environments" from which they could not fight back effectively. More than anything else, this disparity between the relentless maneuvering of Israeli units and the near total lack of maneuver among the Syrians allowed tiny IDF units to smash far larger Syrian forces, which proved the difference between victory and defeat' (Pollack 2004: 506). (IGPO)

Yakhin's tanks, up on their firing ramps, which attacked the first and last vehicles in the column, trapping the rest in a killing field. Private Joseph Zadok, the outpost's bazookaman, witnessed the fight:

> For the whole night we were firing into the convoy that was full of ammunition ... it was a firework show ... Ten times more impressive than the celebrations on Independence Day. In my humble opinion, it was also meaningful to continue fighting. The Syrians experienced a terrible blow there. We were in a valley of death. They tried to rescue the convoy without success, we burned everything. We killed a lot of people. All the valley was covered with hulks of tanks and armored personnel carriers. (Quoted in Kotas-Bar 2013)

Despite such devastation, the Syrian advance didn't seem to be slowing at all. Speaking several days after the battle, one Israeli officer 'still recalled the onslaught in shocked tones: "They flowed in like water, finding their way wherever they had a chance"' (quoted in *Sunday Times* Insight Team 1974: 154). It was bad enough to have so few tanks standing by in defence of his position, but the reality of Elimelech's situation was that he had little hope of artillery support or, perhaps more importantly, air support. There was nowhere near enough artillery to interdict effectively the Syrians' massed formations across the whole front. The IDF had come to rely heavily upon IAF close air support taking up the artillery's slack, but the combination of a SAM screen augmented with ZSU-23-4 radar-guided gunnery was taking a grim toll on the IAF that left the Israeli units on the ground to watch helplessly as their much-needed air support vanished in front of their eyes.

Without the IAF to break up an enemy assault, the outposts were reliant upon the increasingly exhausted tank crews and their own meagre supply of arms. The Syrian attacks continued throughout the new day, with Elimelech calling in to report a new force of infantry dismounting from trucks around 1.5km away and setting out towards Outpost 107 in a skirmish line. Yakhin's tanks, their commanders unwilling to wait for the infantry to come within RPG range, opened fire at about 450m in concert with the outpost's machine guns: 'The forward line of Syrian infantrymen was cut down. Those behind went flat and after a few minutes began to pull back. There had been no attempt by the Syrian infantry at fire and maneuver and no coordination with their tanks, which would soon mount a failed attack from another direction' (Rabinovich 2004: 193). Zadok remembered the determination of the enemy: 'They tried to run at us all the time … But I guess the fatalistic Syrian soldier who made his attack towards us, knew or thought he knew he was going to run into dramatically strong fire power. They didn't know that it wasn't really the case' (quoted in Kotas-Bar 2013).

As the afternoon progressed, Elimelech saw a small force of seven Syrian T-54/55 main battle tanks break off from their main formation and make straight for his outpost. Elimelech's call for help was answered by the arrival of half-a-dozen Ishermans from a rapidly organized home-guard unit and the two sides traded fire with no apparent ill effects, the Syrians eventually breaking off, probably due to a shortage of ammunition. The Ishermans motored off to deal with another of the seemingly never-ending crises that were wracking the whole Israeli line, leaving Elimelech and his men without support apart from Yakhin's original three tanks. As the second evening of the war started to turn towards dusk, the Syrians made another attempt on the outpost: 'A lone Syrian tank approached the bunker complex to provide direct support while a Syrian armoured personnel carrier picked its way through the minefield before stopping to disembark a squad of riflemen, who in their turn fanned out and headed for the wire surrounding the bunker' (Asher & Hammel 1987: 95). Zadok had arrived at the outpost only the morning before, but he rose to his new challenge, irrespective of circumstances. Seizing his bazooka – most likely a Belgian-made 83mm RL-83 Blindicide – but acting without orders and under his own initiative, he made his way across the outpost and then, 'to the total astonishment of his comrades' (Asher & Hammel 1987: 95), moved into open ground outside the compound to get a better shot at the tank, which he promptly destroyed. Zadok's success was compounded by the actions of Sergeant Nissan Avidan, who, opening fire on the Syrian infantry struggling at the wire, quickly cut down five of them, forcing the remainder and their APC to retreat. A short while later another APC approached the post but ran over an anti-tank mine, killing all on board.

As Monday dawned the artillery bombardments continued with the same ferocity they had exhibited since the first moments of the war, and showing no sign of letting up any time soon; Elimelech decided to leave his position in the observation post and look in on his men, sheltering in the main bunker 30m away. Dashing through the trenches as shells burst and shattered around the outpost, he made it to the entrance of the bunker, pausing at its entrance. Gasping for breath and covered in sweat, he lit a cigarette and steadied his breathing:

> only then did he enter with a casual 'How you doing?' He found that his first sergeant had organized a strict regimen in order to keep discipline intact. One-third of the men were preparing for inspection – cleaning weapons, polishing boots, shaving. Another third were on alert status, prepared to rush to their positions if the alarm was sounded. The remainder were sleeping. (Rabinovich 2004: 289–90)

The intensity of the bombardment and the strength of the attacks took their toll on the nerves and spirit of the men; Jacob Hirsch remembered how

Destroyed Syrian armour and bridging vehicles litter the ground around the anti-tank ditch, 13 October 1973, in stark testament both to the aggression of the Syrian advance and to the ferocity of Israeli defensive fire. The bridging units suffered badly at the hands of the Israelis as they made their way towards the anti-tank ditch, with losses mounting at every stage of the ambitious Syrian attack. Only sheer weight of numbers allowed them to punch through the Israeli defences, but at a terrible cost that would tell in the coming days as the chance to turn the advance into a breakthrough faltered and died. (IGPO)

> We did not talk to each other about what would happen if, God forbid, the Syrians get in, but we knew that we had nowhere to go. You couldn't get out alive. It's like being on an island surrounded by sharks that will eat you up. I don't believe that the Syrians, if they'd got into the post, would have spared us. (Quoted in Kotas-Bar 2013)

Yet there was no thought of surrender, symbolized by the desire of the men to keep the Israeli national flag flying, raising it every time it was brought down by the artillery strikes. Hirsch felt that 'It was important for us. Maybe it was instinct, I don't know. We said, first and foremost, to be clear, they know we're not moving. We're here' (quoted in Kotas-Bar 2013).

As the artillery bombardment subsided, Elimelech took stock of their situation and organized a 360-degree perimeter defence as the sheer number of Syrian vehicles and men that had passed by Outpost 107 to the west meant that an attack could come from any angle at any time, from infantry or tanks or both. Apart from the four wall-mounted machine guns and Zadok's bazooka the men were nearly all armed with Uzi submachine guns, which wouldn't be a great deal of use when trading fire with soldiers carrying AKM assault rifles. Nevertheless, they made do, and taking to the walls of the outpost saw a lone Syrian tank making its way towards the outpost when it

> hit a mine 150 yards [135m] away. The explosion threw the tank commander from the turret and killed the others aboard. Instead of fleeing, the survivor ran towards the strongpoint waving a white undershirt…The garrison's astonishment at his safe passage turned to amazement when he shouted in Arabic, 'Ana Shmuel' [I am Shmuel]. The Israelis understood him to be indicating that he was a Jew from Damascus who had been drafted into the Syrian army. He was taken prisoner and eventually sent to the rear, but the garrison never learned whether he was who they thought he was. (Rabinovich 2004: 290)

As Monday drew to a close the situation in the Valley of Tears was reaching its most desperate point, so desperate that Yakhin's tiny tank force received a call from headquarters that sounded like the end for Elimelech and his men: 'Listen, we received orders to retreat back; I hope we'll see you' (quoted in Kotas-Bar 2013). The young officer found it difficult to offer any sort of response: 'I had no words in my mouth. I felt very uncomfortable … now we were actually alone. They had left us. There was no one to consult. The battalion was no help … I realized that I had no place to go. I decided that we were staying at the outpost, come what may. I did not tell anyone' (quoted in Kotas-Bar 2013). He called battalion command on the radio and asked for artillery support; there wasn't any. He asked for air support; there wasn't any. All the battalion could offer was the platitude that 'the nation is behind you' (quoted in Rabinovich 2004: 290), which was small comfort. Elimelech observed how 'You look around and you realize that you are alone. Some say, "Hang on, all of Israel is behind you." You look back and see that everywhere is full of Syrians. Where is Israel?' (quoted in Kotas-Bar 2013).

Some 200m to the north of Outpost 107, what looked like yet another Syrian formation was passing. Hirsch counted them as they went: 'First one, then a second, a third, I lost count at fifty. We watched them pass along in two lines; it felt like I was sitting in the cinema watching films about the world wars. They stop and start, passing to the north of us as we look at them like dummies' (quoted in Kotas-Bar 2013). Elimelech called for artillery support and again for air support, but nothing came except the same empty answers. The realization that there was no help had a profound effect on the young officer:

> When I realized that this was the case … and that there was no one to trust, I changed the way I lived my life. From that moment, it's just me and the Almighty. It is. Nobody tells me what to do or how to do it. It doesn't work. Because today someone can say this and yet tomorrow they'll say something else. You can't rely on trust. That is how I live. (Quoted in Kotas-Bar 2013)

Tuesday started inauspiciously; a Syrian tank that had stopped due to mechanical problems 365m from the outpost made the most of its temporary hiatus by shelling the bunker constantly, wrecking all four of Outpost 107's wall-mounted machine guns, leaving the defenders with a couple of FN FAL *Romats*, a handful of Uzis and Zadok's bazooka. After the tank moved off a quick excursion to the APC that had hit an anti-tank mine on Sunday night provided a number of assault rifles, light machine guns, ammunition and some RPGs, not that such a haul would have been of much use against the latest Syrian onrush. Elements of the 7th and 9th Infantry divisions were combined with a fresh brigade of the 3rd Armoured Division and 70 T-62s from the Presidential Guard to try, once again, to force a way through the Israelis ranged against them.

This last great Syrian attack formed up at the same jumping-off points as the first waves from Saturday, moving along the road a few hundred metres north of Outpost 107, and provided a tempting target. Elimelech ordered his bazookaman to engage the force and so Private Zadok, having seemingly developed a taste for tank-hunting during his Sunday encounter, took his bazooka and destroyed five more tanks in quick succession, saying that he had decided to 'make the most of this ability' (quoted in Kotas-Bar 2013). Such dangerous work didn't faze him, but a short time later he was wounded by tank fire against the outpost – the only soldier under Elimelech's command who was hit throughout the whole ordeal. He recalled the event:

> That shell smashed me completely … I lost blood with every beat of my heart. You know that your situation is terrible, but the trick is to keep silent. The guys were beside me. You mustn't show signs of panic, despite the pressure. You're lying and bleeding, and they look at you, know what your situation is more or less, but you have to keep breathing. (Quoted in Kotas-Bar 2013)

Israeli engineers repair a damaged Centurion main battle tank on the Golan Heights. Throughout the most intense first few days of the Syrian attack the support services of the IDF worked tirelessly, often close to and occasionally among the front lines, actively searching out damaged vehicles; they 'either towed them away for repair or, if possible, repaired them on the spot' (Gal 1986: 161). Of the 250 Israeli tanks that had been damaged or knocked out in the first phase of the war, the engineers managed to return 150 to front-line service within a few days. (IGPO)

As for the Syrian column, it didn't pause or deviate, ignoring the damage caused by Outpost 107, pushing on into the valley.

By Wednesday, battalion headquarters had lost contact with Outpost 107. Fearing the worst, a relief force of three tanks (to be joined on the way by a pair of half-tracks carrying Golani soldiers) was organized under the command of Lieutenant Colonel Yair Nafshi and sent out to relieve the position. Working their way through Kuneitra, the small force 'drove through the part of town closest to the Syrian lines in the belief that the Syrian troops who had penetrated the town would not be expecting an Israeli approach from that direction. Syrian soldiers appeared from side streets and waved at the dust-covered vehicles, assuming they were Syrian. Nafshi, dust-covered himself, waved back' (Rabinovich 2004: 302). Making their way into the compound through a safe route, members of the relief force were astonished to find all the men of Outpost 107 alive, albeit fast asleep from extreme exhaustion. The joy of the relieved was matched by that of the relievers, Gershon Gulzar, one of the outpost's men, recalling how Nafshi shouted at them 'You lions, you lions!' (quoted in Kotas-Bar 2013).

The Syrian attack, broken in the south on Monday, had finally faltered and died in the Valley of Tears on Tuesday. There were awards for Elimelech and for Zadok, the latter's citation telling of how he 'took the initiative, and with his bazooka opened fire at enemy tanks … [and how] he was a model of resourcefulness, courage, composure and devotion to duty' (quoted in Kotas-Bar 2013). Elimelech was awarded a Chief of Staff Citation in recognition of his leadership, but he was in no doubt about the role that Yakhin's force had played in the defence of the outpost: 'Without the tanks we would not have survived' (quoted in Kotas-Bar 2013). Joseph Zadok was fortunate to survive his wounds; he went on to marry, have four children and two grandchildren, acknowledging that 'To come out alive against such odds is truly a miracle … It is my great victory…The Syrians wanted to kill me, to destroy me, to finish me, and I raised a family' (quoted in Kotas-Bar 2013).

Mount Hermon

6–22 October 1973

BACKGROUND TO BATTLE

The three distinct battles that were fought for Mount Hermon, on 6 October, 8 October and 21–22 October respectively, all but spanned the duration of the 1973 war. The intense fighting between some of the best soldiers that either side had to offer would show off the qualities – and shortcomings – of the various Israeli and Syrian units which took part, in some ways becoming a microcosm of some of the larger issues at play throughout the conflict.

The southernmost peak of Mount Hermon had been seized by the Israelis on the last day of the 1967 war, with the rest of the mountain remaining in Syrian hands. A single IAF helicopter had tried to land on the uppermost peak but, due to bad weather, had to settle for a slightly lower landing ground, where it deposited a small force of Golani soldiers who took the mountain – or at least the south-eastern portion of it – for Israel, naming their landing site Mitzpe Shlagim (the Snow Lookout). The strategic value of the position, where 'on a clear day one could see Haifa to the west and the Syrian capital of Damascus to the east' (Herzog 1975: 69), quickly became apparent. In the wake of the 1967 ceasefire the mountain fastness grew into the Israeli anchor point of the northern Golan, providing a peerless observation post across the entire Syrian and Lebanese lines, able to give advance warning of any build-up or attack. It also proved to be an ideal location for a radar position and the gathering of signals and communications

Brigadier General Raphael 'Raful' Eitan commanded the Israeli 36th Armored Division that was tasked with holding the northern sector of the Golan Heights. His command comprised the 188th 'Barak' Armored Brigade (Colonel Yitzhak Ben Shoham); the 7th Armored Brigade (Colonel Avigdor 'Yanush' Ben Gal); the 1st 'Golani' Infantry Brigade (Colonel Amir Drori); and the 31st Parachute Brigade (Colonel Elisha Shelem). An Israeli born and bred, Eitan had enjoyed a long military career up to this point, serving as an officer in the Harel Brigade in the 1948–49 War of Independence, commanding a paratroop battalion during the 1956 Suez crisis, and a paratroop brigade during the 1967 Six-Day War. After his impressive defence of the Golan in 1973 – during a war in which few of the Israeli commanders came through with such unequivocal praise – he would eventually be promoted to Chief of Staff (1978–83), his military career coming to an end in the grey confusion of the Lebanon War of 1982. (IGPO)

intelligence; a highly sophisticated listening post was constructed in the subsequent years, supported by a complex of bunkers and tunnels dug deep into the mountain to ensure that 'the eyes of the nation', as it would become known, would be well defended. At the time of the outbreak of war in October 1973, the outpost was manned by 55 personnel, mostly 'army and air force intelligence personnel and technicians' (Rabinovich 2004: 154), as well as a small detachment of an officer (2nd Lieutenant Hagai Punk) and 13 men from the Golani Brigade's 13th 'Gideon' Battalion, three of whom were detailed to a small observation post around 1.5km away from the main fortification.

The Syrians had made the Israeli post on Mount Hermon something of an intelligence priority, with consistent attempts at espionage that, despite the disruption and arrest of one of the main spy rings responsible, bore important fruit. The trials of the accused revealed that 'Detailed drawings of the entries and exits to the labyrinth of bunkers and connecting corridors, even specifications of the relative strengths of the armor-plated doors and the layouts of surrounding mine fields and booby traps found their way into Syrian hands' (*Sunday Times* Insight Team 1974: 384). Despite such an ominous breach of security, no particular measures seem to have been taken by the Israelis to adapt or augment their defences on the Hermon in direct response; instead, the installation was in the final stages of a period of reconstructive work that saw existing defences temporarily removed, with several features (such as the steel bunker doors) in a state of less than satisfactory repair, and an anti-aircraft battery that had been stationed in defence of the outpost moved down to the Golan only a week before the attack. As the historian Abraham Rabinovich notes, such a casual approach to the security of the most important intelligence and early-warning fortification in the whole of Israel is stark testimony to the hubristic Israeli attitude that they had nothing to fear from the Syrians.

An Israeli soldier points to the wreckage of a downed Syrian fighter-bomber on the Golan near Kuneitra, 11 October 1973. The initial successes of the SyAAF, though costly, hadn't secured them air superiority; the IAF, initially shaken by the toll taken by Soviet-made ZSU-23-4s and SAM anti-aircraft networks, had recovered sufficiently to begin adapting its tactics and fighting back in earnest, launching a massive air offensive on 11 October that attacked airfields and other important installations across Syria. Fierce engagements were fought over the Golan, 'some of them involving between 30 and 60 aircraft. These were fought at altitudes of between 160 ft (50 m) and 20,000 ft (6000 m), and at speeds varying from 125 to 900 mph (200 and 1500 km/h)' (Nicolle & Cooper 2004: 67). Scores of aircraft were damaged or lost, with the Syrians definitely suffering the worst of it at the hands of the more experienced, better-trained Israeli pilots. (IGPO)

On the evening of Wednesday 3 October, Colonel Najib Suleiman Hassan, the commander of the highly regarded 500-strong Syrian 82nd Parachute Battalion, was holding a conference with his commanders. After the close of their summer training manoeuvres his unit had not returned to base, but had instead been detailed to take up a holding position in the vicinity of Mount Hermon. His command was augmented by two further companies, one of them a special weapons company that included men trained in the use of 9M14 *Malyutka* (AT-3) ATGMs and 9K32 *Strela-2* (SA-7) shoulder-launched anti-aircraft missiles. They were making the final preparations for their surprise attack on the isolated Israeli outpost, an attack that called for an infantry and helicopter-borne assault that would quickly surround the base, cutting it off from help or reinforcement. The men who were to undertake the attack had been well briefed about the defences of the complex, and each unit had been given well thought-through objectives, being told 'what to attack and how to attack it' (O'Ballance 1979: 129). The Syrians understood the value of the prize that was on offer, and had detailed arguably the best-trained and most capable unit in the Syrian Army for its capture.

For the Israelis, the fact that their nation's most advanced surveillance outpost was almost entirely unaware of and unprepared for the coming Syrian storm was almost beyond irony. On Friday 5 October, the day before the attack, the soldiers and technicians of the mountain outpost carried on as usual, despite the increasing realization within some sectors of the Israeli high command that something might be very, very wrong. Alerts were starting to be issued, but none apparently came through to the headquarters of the Golani Brigade, nor to the Hermon outpost. There was a plan in place, should such an alert have been received, to despatch a 14-man section of reinforcements to the fortification, but instead the soldiers and workers on the mountain remained unsupported. They observed the vast build-up of Syrian

A Syrian Army T-34-85 medium tank sits at the top of Mount Hermon, near the waterfall at Wadi Saar, one of three sources of the Jordan River, April 1971. Though obsolescent in 1967, the T-34-85 was still to be found in second-line units and especially as localized support for defensive strongpoints (the Golani Brigade came across several such examples during their attack on Tel Azaziat and Tel Faher on 9 June 1967). The tank's 85mm ZiS-S-53 gun may have been a poor match against Israeli Centurions, but it could be effective against the M50 Sherman and would still wreak havoc on M3 half-tracks or infantry formations. (Photo by Frances M. Ginter/Getty Images)

armour on the plains below, reported it, and then continued about their day more or less as usual. A brief alert that evening caused the men to retreat within the bunker, sealing the steel doors, but when the morning came they all returned to the casual behaviour of the preceding days: 'On the morning of Yom Kippur the observation posts were as usual manned: routine reconnaissance along the approaching routes took place; but many of the soldiers remained in the synagogue to pray' (Herzog 1975: 72).

Knocked-out Syrian vehicles on the Golan, with a wrecked BTR-152 APC in the foreground, 13 October 1973. Capable of carrying 18 troops (with two crew), the BTR-152's open top made it vulnerable, but it was still considerably better than the alternative of soft-skinned vehicles. Syrian mechanized infantry followed the general Soviet practice of remaining in the APC during combat, using it as a firing platform for their small arms. The lack of tactical training, knowledge and flexibility among their commanders, however, meant that Syrian mechanized infantry never succeeded in working as part of a combined-arms team with their armour. (IGPO)

MAP KEY

1   1445hrs, 6 October: Syria's 82nd Parachute Battalion and elements of the 183rd Commando Battalion assault the Israeli positions on the Hermon, on foot from the 'Syrian' Hermon and by helicopter insertion on the mountain's southern slopes. After a series of brief but bloody engagements, the outpost falls.

2   8 October: An infantry and armoured column from the Golani Brigade attempt to retake the Hermon and are rebuffed with serious casualties.

3   21 October: Operation *Kinuach* ('Dessert'), a joint attack on the Hermon is launched by the Golani Brigade and Israeli paratroopers: the 17th Training Battalion attacks from the west, the 51st Battalion and the Sayeret Golani attack from the south, while the 317th Parachute Brigade attacks from the north.

4   22 October: The Syrian positions on the Hermon are overrun, with the Israelis capturing the mountain.

Battlefield environment

Mount Hermon (Jebel Sheikh in Arabic) lies at the northernmost tip of the Israeli-controlled Golan Heights; it constitutes the southernmost edge of the Anti-Lebanon mountain range, bordered by Lebanon to the west and Syria to the east. The mountain itself runs from north-east to south-west and comprises three roughly equivalent peaks about half a kilometre distant from one another, the 'Syrian' Hermon being in the north while the 'Israeli' Hermon lies to the south. At a height of 2,814m above sea level, Mount Hermon provides excellent views of the surrounding lands, including Lebanon all the way to the Mediterranean coast, the Hula valley and the plains of Galilee, the whole of the Golan Heights, and a significant portion of south-west Syria including the capital Damascus some 42km away, which can be made out clearly with the naked eye. The 'Syrian' Hermon was slightly higher than both the Mitzpe Shlagim peak of 2,224m and the slightly lower 'Israeli' Hermon on which the observation outpost had been built, which was at an elevation of 2,208m above sea level.

The mountain was difficult to approach, with only one main road nearby, running roughly east to west from Banias and Dan to Masada. Another small road had been built as a spur from the Banias–Masada road, running north up to the southern slopes of the Israeli Hermon to facilitate the development of a ski lift in 1971. As well as the main outpost, several smaller observation posts were dotted around the mountain. As for the main base itself, which was comprised of two above-ground levels and an underground bunker complex, it 'jutted out like a squat tower on the peak. It was well-built, but the upper system of fortification on the lower building had not yet been completed. There were signs of negligence: the main gate of the position had been damaged and swung open on its hinges unrepaired; no communication trenches had been dug around the main fortification … Northern Command had never estimated that this position would be the object of a major Syrian assault because it was not on a major axis of advance. It could only be an object for routine raids. The fortifications were built to withstand artillery fire and Air Force bombing, but the trench system which would enable the infantry to fight effectively had not been completed' (Herzog 1975: 69–72).

This view looks towards the main Israeli position on Mount Hermon. The rough and irregular terrain was similar in many aspects to that found on the rest of the Golan, with rough scree and irregular rocky outcroppings making any approaches up the mountain difficult, dangerous and time-consuming. There was little vegetation to provide cover on the upper slopes, just an abundance of loose, treacherous rock covering the ravines and gullies that scored the surface of the mountain. The road, narrow, winding and treacherous for armoured vehicles, runs south from the crest of the mountain down to the Banias–Masada road. (Dr. Avishai Teicher)

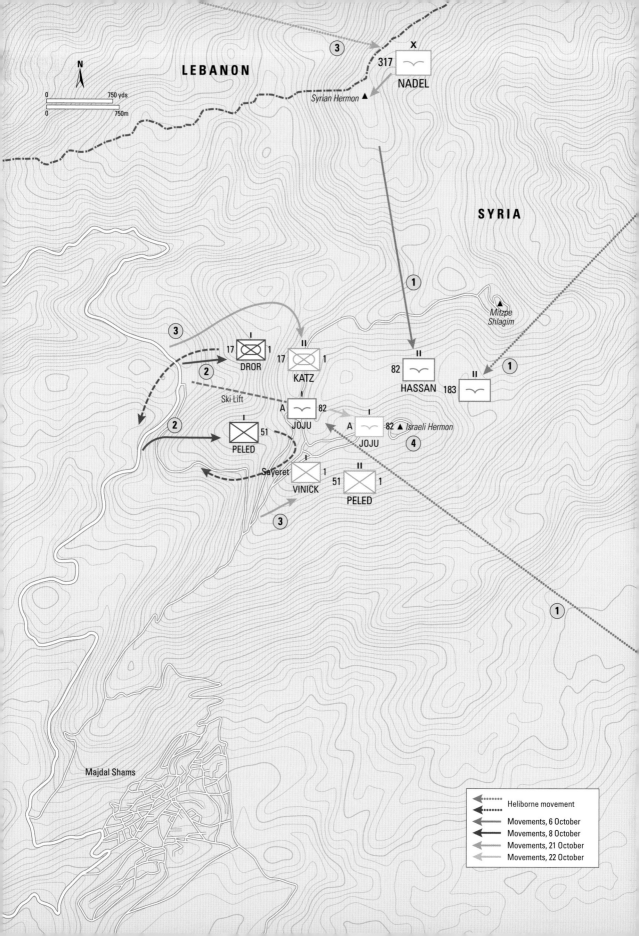

LEBANON

N

0   750 yds
0   750 m

③ ─── 317 ⊠ X
NADEL

▲ Syrian Hermon

SYRIA

① ↓

▲ Mitzpe Shlagim

③

17 ⊠ I 1
DROR

II
17 ⊠ 1
KATZ

II
82 ⌣
HASSAN

II
183 ⌣

①

②

Ski Lift

A ⌣ 82
JOJU

A I 82
JOJU ▲ Israeli Hermon

④

②

I
51 ⊠
PELED

Sayeret

I
⊠ 1
VINICK

II
51 ⊠ 1
PELED

③

Majdal Shams

⋯◄	Heliborne movement
◄▬	Heliborne movement
◄───	Movements, 6 October
◄───	Movements, 8 October
◄───	Movements, 21 October
◄───	Movements, 22 October

INTO COMBAT

As the small group of observers on Mount Hermon looked down at the Syrian positions on the Golan at 1345hrs on Saturday 6 October, they saw Syrian troops pulling camouflage nets from their guns. Almost immediately shellfire started raining down on the mountain top, driving the Israelis from their positions down into the safety of the bunkers. The artillery bombardment was so intense that any attempt to man the external observation posts was impossible; 2nd Lieutenant Punk sent a signal to Northern Command explaining that they were under artillery attack, but his comment that the situation was under control and that they would repair the post's aerials after the bombardment stopped indicated that the defenders didn't understand that the artillery barrage was merely the overture.

The Syrian attack was meant to have gone in at 'S Hour' (1400hrs) on 6 October, but some last-minute hitches in organization meant that the men of the 82nd Parachute Battalion only received their final orders at 1200hrs. Lieutenant Ahmed Rifai al-Joju, commander of A Company, set out with his troops at 1400hrs in four Mi-8 helicopters, their task being to land 'half a mile from the Israeli structure and [to] take positions covering the outpost and the single road leading up to it from the Golan' (Rabinovich 2004: 154); then they would cut off any relief from the Masada road and provide supporting fire from the rest of the battalion which was to advance on foot from the 'Syrian' Hermon down to the 'Israeli' Hermon, thus catching the defenders in simultaneous attacks from the north and south. Al-Joju's force lost a helicopter on the approach, its rotors clipping the edge of the mountain as it came in to land, but the remaining Mi-8s delivered their men without any problems. The Syrians immediately engaged the small outpost at the top of the ski lift, the heavy machine gun of which quickly jammed, forcing the troops there to abandon their position and escape down the mountain.

By 1445hrs the Syrians advancing from the north had come within 200m of the outpost. Captain Jassam al Salah, in command of the leading Syrian company, noted how it seemed that 'the door to the Israeli position [was] wide open' (quoted in Asher & Hammel 1987: 146). A quick frontal assault was launched in the hope of overcoming the defenders with shock and overwhelming numbers, and it might have worked; the artillery barrage had knocked out two of the post's three heavy machine guns, and the defenders were mostly armed with nothing better than Uzis. Nevertheless, the Israelis put up a significant defence, with the initial Syrian attack beaten back with around 50 casualties when it was barely 90m shy of the Israeli position. The battle degenerated into an exchange of fire, one that favoured the attackers with their superior numbers and better weapons; the Syrians started advancing with greater care, moving in small groups from cover, all the while supported by sniper fire.

The Syrian tactics started to tell, with growing numbers of Israelis wounded (including Punk, shot in the shoulder) or killed until there were only half-a-dozen men fighting off scores of determined Syrians. In the assault the officers of the two lead attacking companies, Captain Salah and Captain Mahmoud Ma'aleh, were both wounded, but this didn't seem to impair the cohesion or drive of the Syrian attack, which was pressed home with relentless inevitability. The Syrians were well camouflaged and difficult to spot, one of the defenders noting how their positions could 'be gauged only by the flare of

their gunfire' (quoted in Asher & Hammel 1987: 146). By 1700hrs the Syrian paratroopers launched a surprise rush attack from the west, which succeeded in breaking into the outer defences and forced the small band of defenders to retreat into the bunker. Lieutenant David Nachliel recalled: 'We retreated into the hall where we took shelter at the beginning of the artillery bombardment. We blocked all the possible openings for [*sic*] the event that the enemy would come. The enemy entered the post and began clearing the tunnels and rooms with hand grenades, with their personal weapon[s], and with smoke grenades' (quoted in Shaked 2014).

The situation for the Israelis inside the bunker complex was confused and frightening; the survivors were scattered in a variety of rooms or communication tunnels, with all sense of cohesion lost. The silence would be shattered by the detonation of Syrian grenades dropped down air ducts as the attackers started to force their way into the complex, room by room. The small force that had been the last to withdraw into the bunker retreated into a communication tunnel, throwing grenades to keep at bay any Syrians who approached, but the situation was dire; by 2100hrs the generator had been knocked out, the defenders had no contact with the outside world, they were surrounded by hundreds of Syrians who were making their way through the whole complex with a grim inevitability, and all they had to defend themselves were their Uzis with only a single magazine apiece. The officers, led by Lieutenant Gadi Zidover, the commander of the outpost, decided that escape was the only option, and so after gathering together all those they could find a small group of 20 Israelis made their way out of the fortification.

The small band made it to the darkness outside and slipped through a portion of perimeter fence that had been destroyed in the initial Syrian attack. After about 90 minutes the Israelis reached the upper portion of the ski lift,

An officer hands out mail from home to Israeli soldiers who are relaxing in one of the forward positions on Mount Hermon, on or around 11 October 1973. By this time the Syrian assaults in central and southern Golan had faltered, fought to a standstill by a thin and desperate line of Israeli armour that forced the Syrian divisions to withdraw back towards their jumping-off points, but in the far north Mount Hermon was still firmly in Syrian hands. An initial attempt to retake the outpost by soldiers of the Golani Brigade had been bloodily rebuffed in the first few days of the war, but the shame of the loss – felt deeply by both the military high command, and by the Golani Brigade who had twice been defeated by the Syrians on the same ground – as well as the strategic importance of the post, meant that another attempt to retake it was inevitable. (IGPO)

A pair of Israeli soldiers pass the time of day, with the wrecked outpost of the 'Israeli' Hermon in the background. The fall of the outpost would prove to be an intelligence bonanza for the Syrians and, by extension, their Soviet backers. Abraham Rabinovich noted how 'Soviet experts who arrived to dismantle the electronic equipment were exultant to discover most of it intact. For the Syrians, the information elicited from Israeli intelligence personnel in interrogation would prove an even greater windfall' (Rabinovich 2004: 155). (IGPO)

where they suddenly came under murderous fire from less than 200m – they had walked straight into the path of al-Joju's company which had been positioned in groups to ambush any attempted relief efforts from the Golan below. The Israelis scattered, with at least one, Lieutenant David Nachliel, charging his ambushers while he fired his Uzi from the hip; such boldness worked in his favour and he made it through, meeting up with two more survivors as well as Punk, whereupon they fell into another ambush in which they were shot at and bombarded with grenades. They ran pell-mell down the hill, taking cover in dead ground where available, finally gaining their own lines, but only after being shot at by one of their own Centurion tanks for good measure. Of the 55 men in the outpost, 31 were taken prisoner and four were killed in its defence; 20 had escaped, 11 of whom eventually made it back to their own lines, the remainder having been killed as they tried to flee the mountain. As Abraham Rabinovich noted, 'The fall of the Hermon was for Israel the single most humiliating episode of the Yom Kippur War. From the Golani Brigade to the General Staff, a grim determination took shape to regain it at any price' (Rabinovich 2004: 155).

Colonel Amir Drori, commander of the Golani Brigade, wanted to launch an immediate attack in the hope of relieving those still trapped in the bunker, but he was overruled by Brigadier General Eitan. Major General Yitzhak Hofi, responsible for the whole of Northern Command, also wanted the Hermon retaken as soon as practicable, but the intense strain on the Israeli positions on the Golan – there were too many holes to plug, and far too few troops and tanks with which to plug them – made an immediate attempt impossible. Nevertheless, the following day Hofi, after receiving reports (erroneous, as it happened) that there was still a small force of Israelis fighting on the Hermon, decided to force the issue and gave Drori orders to retake the position at once.

The Syrians, expecting an Israeli counter-attack almost from the moment they launched their own attack, had been busy working on their defences. Al-Joju spent the afternoon of Sunday 7 October carefully positioning his men along the Hermon's rough terrain, thus ensuring that an Israeli counter-attack would have to pay a heavy price for any gains made:

> The narrow roadway was mined along the length of a curve that would prevent attackers from bringing adequate firepower to bear. The commandos were deployed well away from the roadway itself, in individual fighting positions from which they could cover a very narrow front with RPGs, machine guns, hand grenades, and their personal weapons. Any attacker attempting to outflank the Syrian defensive block would have to operate while silhouetted against the skyline. (Asher & Hammel 1987: 146)

Drori's force comprised around 150 men in two columns, one mechanized and the other on foot. The mechanized column, which was to be responsible for the main thrust of the attack, was drawn from the Golani's 17th Training Battalion, an NCO training unit, and consisted of a number of half-tracks supported by two tanks and a bulldozer led by the 17th Training Battalion's commanding officer, Lieutenant Colonel Dubi 'Dov' Dror; the foot column consisted of a force of Golani soldiers from the 51st Battalion led by their newly promoted commander, Major Yehuda Peled, with a few teams from Sayeret Golani, the Golani Brigade's reconnaissance unit. The armoured column advanced north along the narrow, winding road with Peled's infantry moving on a different axis, climbing up the Hermon from the west. As the units inched their way up the mountain they were effectively blinded by the heavy morning mist that still lay thick upon the ground. The armoured column came upon the narrow curve in the road that al-Joju had chosen for an ambush

An Israeli PA-18 Super Cub, usually used by the IAF as a training aircraft, is seen here in an aerial-reconnaissance role, flying low near an Israeli armoured column that is advancing across the Golan during the Six-Day War. With the capture of the Hermon outpost in the first hours of the 1973 war, the Israelis had lost their best, most advanced observation platform. From the Hermon the whole of the Golan, as well as the approaches to it from Syria, could be observed, and the value of such an asset in spotting enemy troop movements and plotting interdictory artillery fire was sorely missed by the Israelis. (IGPO)

Yehuda Peled

Major Yehuda Peled, commander of the Golani Brigade's 51st Battalion, was born in the Kibbutz Yagur in 1940. He joined the IDF in 1960, a year after his brother, a paratrooper, had been killed in a border incident near Egypt; opting to go into the Golani Brigade, Peled found the aggressive nature of the outfit to his liking, completing courses in officer training that led to his appointment as a platoon commander in Sayeret Golani. Badly wounded in Operation *Swallow* (an incursion onto the Golan Heights) in 1962, he was released from service and returned to his kibbutz, only to be called back on the eve of the 1967 war – as a reserve officer he was detailed to the 2nd 'Carmeli' Brigade's reconnaissance company, fighting on the Golan during that war's short campaign. He returned to the regular forces in 1970, becoming the commanding officer of Sayeret Golani for two years before completing a staff college course that saw him promoted to major and given command of the 51st Battalion on 4 October 1973, 48 hours before the start of the war. Peled was in charge of the small infantry force during the first abortive attempt to retake the Hermon on 8 October, getting much further than the armoured column that tried to force its way up the mountain's thin and winding road. On 21 October, Peled returned to the Hermon with his battalion, again marching up the hill on foot and fighting bloody engagements against the paratroopers of the 82nd Parachute Battalion, and becoming – like most of his officers – one of the casualties when he was shot through the chest in the early morning. Evacuated off the mountain, he survived the battle and the war and remained in the IDF, playing a role in the Entebbe International Airport hostage-rescue mission of 4 July 1976 and the Lebanon War of 1982, retiring as a brigadier general in 1992.

whereupon Dror's half-track promptly hit a mine, setting off a vicious firefight. The front of the Israeli column was battered by gunfire and anti-tank weapons, but the road was too narrow – and the ground either side of it too rough – to allow the tanks, bringing up the rear of the column, to make their way forward and add their much-needed support to the developing firefight.

Peled's infantry assault had also encountered stiff resistance from the Syrians about a third of the way up the mountain, firing from their well-sited positions. Rabinovich notes how

> Golani rifle fire at two hundred yards proved ineffective, the curve of the tracer bullets showing Peled how their flight was being bent by the powerful wind. Seeking to close range, he ordered his light mortars to fire smoke shells. Clouds scudding along the slope provided additional cover as the troops bounded up from boulder to boulder. At fifty meters, Uzis proved effective. (Rabinovich 2004: 254)

Bit by bit, Peled's men pushed the Syrians back up the slope, eventually gaining the crest of the hill, but his force had suffered two dead and eight wounded in the process. For the armoured column progress had stalled at the curve in the road, with the numbers of dead and wounded rising; the half-tracks and tanks were going nowhere. After three hours of mostly fruitless fighting, Drori decided to abandon the attack; even though Peled had come close to the summit, he hadn't anywhere near enough troops to make an effective attack upon a stronghold held by several hundred Syrians, and there would no help from the now-bloodied armoured column. The heavy mist also precluded accurate air support and artillery fire, thus forcing Drori's hand. The force of around 150 men retreated down the mountain, with a total of 25 dead and 57 wounded – a casualty rate of around 50 per cent – including the commander of the 17th Training Battalion, Lieutenant Colonel Dror. Boldness had not been enough.

Ahmed Rifai al-Joju

Lieutenant Ahmed Rifai al-Joju, commander of the 82nd Parachute Battalion's A Company, would play an important role in all three battles on the Hermon; his troops would cut off access to and from the Israeli outpost in the first moments of the attack, and the defensive lines held by his men on 8 and 21–22 October would inflict heavy casualties on the attacking Golani soldiers. Prior to the surprise attack on the Hermon, al-Joju had been conducting reconnaissance on the Israeli position, and not for the first time; he and his men had previously engaged in secret cross-border incursions to gather intelligence, and now they were busy practising the laying of mines and the setting of ambushes – they didn't know why, but they knew something different was coming. Though little is known about al-Joju, like a number of officers in the 82nd (and presumably the 183rd) he most likely received special training in the Soviet Union from members of their elite units,

concentrating on tactics and the utilization of special weapons. In addition, he was experienced in airborne operations, fighting behind enemy lines and participating in mountain combat. Training was a large part of his schedule, far more so than for a regular officer, and he can be regarded as a thoroughly professional soldier – not a common distinction in the Syrian Army. The men of the 82nd Parachute Battalion were the best-trained, and almost certainly the best-led Syrian troops that took the field in 1973, as they were to prove to the Israelis on several occasions. The final battle for the Hermon saw al-Joju's company defending the crest of the hill against Major Peled's advancing Golani infantry, where they inflicted grievous casualties on Israeli officers and men alike. Eventually, after putting up stiff and bloody resistance for most of the night and early morning of 21–22 October, al-Joju escaped back into Syria with an unknown number of other paratroopers.

The wildly intense battles which had developed in the centre of the Golan plateau precluded any serious further attempt at an Israeli recapture, and when the tide began to turn on Thursday 11 October the main obsession of Northern Command was to launch a counter-attack into Syria as fast and as hard as possible. That campaign proved to be an initial success as the Syrians, their forces grievously damaged by their costly assaults into the Golan, fell back in the face of highly aggressive Israeli armoured attacks. A similar scenario was playing itself out in the Sinai, where, after their initial reverses, the Israelis managed to pull themselves together and start to take a real toll on the Egyptians. As the days passed, both sides realized that a ceasefire brokered by the UN was looming, and so military strategy became the conscious servant of political expediency. As part of that approach, the need to retake the Hermon was crucial; if it wasn't in Israeli hands by the time of the ceasefire there was simply no way that the Syrians would allow its negotiated return. With the war coming to its close, and with the resources finally to hand, the time to strike had come, IDF Chief of Staff David Elazar stating 'I want the Hermon within forty-eight hours' (quoted in Rabinovich 2004: 437).

Kinuach ('Dessert') was the name of the operation; the forces responsible for the recapture of the Hermon were to be Drori's Golani Brigade (comprised of reinforced versions of the same units which had failed on 8 October: Major Yehuda Peled's 51st Battalion; the brigade's reconnaissance company, Sayeret Golani, led by Major Shmaryahu Vinick; and the 17th Training Battalion led by Major David Katz) and Colonel Chaim Nadel's 317th Parachute Brigade. The 51st Battalion was to make an assault on the steep western face of the mountain towards the 'Israeli' Hermon, with the Sayeret Golani on the same approach but further to the left; once the infantry had gained the heights, an armoured column of the 17th Training Battalion fronted by half-a-dozen tanks would advance up the road from the south. Nadel's paratroopers were

to strike at the 'Syrian' Hermon, capturing the strongpoint and cutting off any route of resupply or escape for the Syrians occupying the Israeli positions. Despite the planning and preparations there were still many unknowns, mainly concerning the strength and dispositions of the Syrian defenders. Peled mentioned his somewhat rueful assessment of the operation to Drori: 'This is either going to be very easy, or very hard' (quoted in Rabinovich 2004: 448).

The Syrians had no intention of giving up without a fight. The 82nd Parachute Battalion, responsible for the capture of the mountain, was joined by the 183rd Commando Battalion, another independent special-operations unit, along with several supporting companies, in a defensive ring around the old Israeli outpost (they didn't occupy the structure itself), as well as two companies of Syrian infantry defending the 'Syrian' Hermon. The Syrian positions had undergone significant artillery bombardment in the preceding days, but the barrages resulted in only a few minor casualties, the Syrians being so well dug in. There were more than twice as many Syrians on the Hermon as the Israelis were expecting.

At 1730hrs on 21 October, the two paratrooper battalions of Israel's 317th Parachute Brigade (the 471st and 567th), 625 men in all, were helicoptered in 27 sorties to their positions a little below the crest of the 'Syrian' Hermon, from where they began their advance. It was a textbook exercise; the paratroopers moved with deliberate care through the obstacles and over the rough ground of the mountain as they made for their objectives. Short, sharp firefights that ended in Syrian routs were the order of the day, with only one Israeli paratrooper killed and four wounded. By 0300hrs on the morning of 22 October, the road to the 'Syrian' Hermon had been cut, columns of Syrian reinforcements had been beaten back, and the peak itself had been shelled remorselessly and then stormed by the paratroopers, who discovered that its occupiers had already made off into the night. For the Golani men to the south, however, it was a very different story.

The 400 soldiers of the Golani Brigade began their climb up the western slope at around 1900hrs on 21 October, their advance covered by a rolling artillery barrage that had to be lifted when the shells started hitting a little too close to the leading edge of the Israeli line. The advance was extremely hard work, with each man carrying a 34kg pack, struggling up difficult terrain in the dark, fearful of the eruption of a firefight that could come at any moment.

The Israelis advanced across the ground on which they had fought al-Joju's men previously, surprised to find that the Syrians had abandoned their old positions. The Israeli battalion continued up the mountain, Drori pulling his companies closer together as they approached the summit, when at 0238hrs the mysteriously absent Syrians suddenly opened fire. Equipped with the latest Soviet night 'scopes, the defenders were able to choose their moment, and they made it tell, with many Golani soldiers falling wounded or dead. A Golani trooper recalled how 'On top the Syrians had a warm welcome for us. In every nook and cranny, they had not one but seven snipers. In the first light we suddenly found ourselves at arm's length with them. We actually had fist fights. Everyone was shouting at everyone. Then there was a Syrian air attack' (quoted in *Sunday Times* Insight Team 1974: 385).

The Israeli armoured column, moving on the road some way away, lost most of its tank commanders to snipers, while the lead Centurion and several half-tracks were rapidly knocked-out by well-used anti-tank weapons. As the fight progressed, Drori was shot through the chest; he insisted to the officers remaining that 'You've got to finish this business. Don't dare go down without taking the mountain' (quoted in Rabinovich 2004: 450). Shortly afterwards, Peled was also hit and evacuated; the men now lacked strong direction and fought more by instinct than any tactical plan, battling through the Syrian positions one by one throughout the night and into the dawn. One Golani who took part in the attack recalled the skill of the Syrian defenders:

> The snipers used the classic trick of raising helmets on a stick to draw our fire; they had made positions for themselves around the fort, not in it. Most of them were lying down; they used telescopic sights, and the sun was behind them – right in our eyes. They threw grenades at anything that moved; many of our wounded were from grenade fragments. (Quoted in *Sunday Times* Insight Team 1974: 385)

For many of the Israeli soldiers the intensity of the fighting was shocking; Benny Masas remembered how 'I was never shot at before. I was in a raid before. People fired and fired and fired, but gunfire like it was on the Hermon I never saw before. I was also in Gaza when we ran into a terrorist. It was over very quickly, not like what happened here' (quoted in Shaked 2014).

The Israeli attack, given new focus by the brigade operations officer, continued with renewed vigour; the fight dragged on into the morning, but Syrian resistance was weakening, either through casualties or from a possible order to withdraw (the truth of the matter is unclear), despite the commander's earlier injunction that his men should 'resist to the death' (quoted in O'Ballance 1979: 213). Whatever the reason, by 1100hrs on 22 October the Hermon was back in Israeli hands. The cost to the Golani Brigade was very high, with 55 dead and 79 wounded. Syrian losses were estimated at 50–60 dead, with 62 prisoners taken.

Analysis

The Six-Day War set the pattern for Israeli and Syrian military development over the next six years, and the assumptions and conclusions that each side drew from that conflict would have significant consequences for both in 1973. For the Israelis the fight on the Golan in 1967 was over in 26 hours, the entire Syrian front crumbling with indecent haste. Such a collapse obscured several notable issues, however: the Syrians, as they showed at Tel Faher and several other sites on the Golan, were not necessarily pushovers. When defending in well-prepared positions they fought with bravery and a stubbornness that showed itself in the growing number of Israeli casualties. The Syrian disintegration of the second day was due in part to Israeli tactical strength, but it also had a lot to do with the dire leadership provided by the Syrian officer corps that intensified tactical and strategic blunders. Kenneth Pollack notes that 'Syrian forces performed poorly at nearly every level. Perhaps the only Syrian personnel who can be excused for the defeat were the actual soldiers,

Near Kuneitra, an Israeli rounds up some defeated Syrian infantry whose value as POWs would be significant. For the IDF, bringing all its soldiers home was a matter of intense commitment, almost irrespective of cost, which led to quickly negotiated prisoner exchanges after the conclusion of hostilities that can seem to the outside observer as having been almost ridiculously one-sided; for example, the historian Reuven Gal notes how in the aftermath of the Six-Day War the Israelis exchanged 591 Syrian POWs for one Israeli pilot and the bodies of two dead soldiers, while after the Yom Kippur War the rate of exchange was 392 Syrians for 65 Israelis and 8,400 Egyptians for 232 Israelis (Gal 1986: 238). (IGPO)

Israelis soldiers sit atop a freshly captured Syrian Army T-62 on the Golan, 13 October 1973. Though visually very similar to the T-55 in a number of ways, the T-62 was built around a larger and more effective 115mm smoothbore gun, and was equipped with night-vision equipment that would cause no small amount of consternation to the Israelis when they encountered it. Despite such advantages the Syrian T-62s fared little better than the T-54/55s, in part because of the extremely high quality of Israeli tank gunnery, it not being unusual for IDF gunners to be able to 'accurately hit moving targets at an impressive range of 2.5 miles [4km]' (Creveld 2002: 161). When such potent gunnery was combined with well-sited firing platforms that had meticulously plotted fields of fire, the result was significant numbers of Syrian vehicles being destroyed at almost unfeasible ranges before they even had a chance to enter combat. The dismal level of Syrian tactical training meant that tank companies, even when they came within range of their foe, would often advance in waves with little or no manoeuvre, thus providing excellent targets for the more flexible Israelis. (IGPO)

artillerymen, and tankers who fought with great bravery and determination and did everything asked of them, only to have nearly every rung of their leadership betray them' (Pollack 2004: 469). Some Syrian officers refused to counter-attack, even though their units were fresh, while others – including General Ahmad al-Mir, the man in charge of the front – simply ran away, al-Mir doing so on a horse all the way back to Damascus, which leavened the tragedy with a healthy dose of bathos. For many junior officers, like Captain Muhammad 'Ammar who had fought in the battles around Tel Faher, the Syrian Army ceased to be a coherent entity: 'The forces that were supposed to block the enemy's advance pulled out without authorization, without coordination. We knew nothing, and had no choice but to fall back. In my platoon alone we had ten killed and four wounded. We had no ammunition and no way of getting more' (quoted in Oren 2002: 301).

Most of the lessons that the Israelis could have learned were drowned out by the rapturous noise of victory. The contemptuous view of the Syrian soldier was exemplified by an Israeli lieutenant – 'They ran like rabbits' (*Newsweek* 1968: 290) – and was probably exacerbated by the fact that there was an abiding enmity between the two sides. Reuven Gal's assessment of the Israeli view on the Six-Day War covers most of the issues:

> The definitive victory was so overwhelming to the Israeli military that it resulted in frequent denial of obvious problems … the Israelis downplayed the fact that their success on the ground was all possible because of the lack of air threat to them. They further overemphasized the role of their armored forces in their victory and thus in the future would concentrate their buildup around tanks to the detriment of the infantry and artillery. More than anything else, the Israeli commanders tended to credit the victory to their own ingenuity rather than at least partially acknowledging the enemy's poor performance. (Gal 1986: 18)

Israeli armoured doctrine had significant flaws, one of the most serious being poor combined-arms integration; the victories in 1967 were achieved despite such flaws, and would lead the Israelis radically to underestimate the need for supporting infantry formations, and to a prejudice against the infantry arm

A badly wounded Israeli soldier is evacuated by helicopter. The 1973 war would leave 2,680 IDF personnel dead and at least 7,000 wounded. The toll among front-line officers, with their 'follow me' ethos, was particularly high, with 28.5 per cent (approximately 1,300 men) becoming casualties. The historian Michael Oren notes: 'each Yom Kippur yields an outpouring of public grief over the battlefield deaths of more than 2,500 Israeli soldiers – the equivalent, in current per capita terms, of 230,000 Americans – and the maiming of vastly more' (Oren 2013). For the Syrians an accurate accounting of their losses suffered was hampered by the traditional secrecy of the state, no doubt compounded by embarrassment at their relatively poor performance in the war; estimates range from around 3,100 dead and 6,000 wounded up to Edward Luttwak and Dan Horowitz's assumption of 'in excess of 12,000 killed' (Luttwak & Horowitz 1975: 392). The truth, however grim, probably lies somewhere in between. (IGPO)

in general. The men of the Golani Brigade displayed many of the impressive qualities for which the IDF was becoming renowned: initiative, aggressiveness, good unit cohesion in combat, delegation to and trust of subordinates, extremely strong leadership – often from the front – at all levels, and an adaptable and opportunistic approach to battle. In many ways the model for such an approach to warfighting was to be found in the *Auftragstaktik* (mission command) of the Wehrmacht of World War II, and it produced similar levels of casualties among NCOs and junior officers. Nevertheless, the 'follow me' ethos was cemented by the examples given and the victories it garnered.

The Yom Kippur War of 1973 demonstrated to some degree the cost of Israeli hubris as well as the significant lessons the Syrians had learned – as well as those they had not. The greatest impact was caused by the surprise nature of the attack; a strategic failure on a monumental scale for the Israeli state. On the Golan the Syrians showed just how seriously they had taken the redevelopment of their army: they displayed a panoply of new weapon systems, from man-portable ATGMs through to highly capable SAM networks; and they fielded an entirely rejuvenated army that was mechanized to an impressive degree, and which had at its core a significant armoured element that, on numbers alone, should have been able to annihilate the Israelis.

The Syrian soldier had also improved. Zeev Schiff, writing in the newspaper *Haaretz* on 30 October 1973, observed a greater aggressiveness among the Arab soldiers:

> We noticed that the Arab fighter improved in several matters: his field tactics gave the impression of being good and coherent, despite the fact that they were doctrinal and inflexible; preparation of the forces was more profound, and the training they went through was apparent. These forces broke through into fields which they had not entered before, such as night combat and effective employment of armour in large numbers in the dark … It was possible to notice improvements over the past in Arab technical command of the arms and weapon systems they possessed … Their combative spirit was better, they even displayed a spirit of sacrifice in many instances. (Quoted in Shoufani 1975: 193)

The very best examples were to be found in the men of the 82nd Parachute Battalion, whose assault on and subsequent defence of the Hermon proved the worth of a well-trained Syrian soldier.

Despite such improvements, two critical flaws remained. The first was the generally poor training of the Syrian troops in mechanized warfare and combined-arms combat – a failing that covered both the infantry and the tank crews, and which led to disastrous tactical mistakes. Kenneth Pollack considered the overall Syrian strategic display rather good, but he is damning when it comes to their tactical performance: 'By and large, Syrian forces performed extremely poorly against the highly skilled Israelis. More than anything else, this huge imbalance between Syrian incompetence and Israeli hypercompetence led inexorably to Syria's defeat. At every turn, the limitations of Syrian tactical performances forced their strategic leadership to work harder to achieve modest successes and turned even minor strategic mistakes into catastrophes' (Pollack 2004: 505–06). Such failings are perhaps understandable when one considers the cultural, intellectual and technical enormity of the leap forward that the Syrian Army was expected to make in a very short space of time, but the costs were very high. Lieutenant Zvika Greengold, one of the heroes of the Golan, put it succinctly: 'They had a great many tanks, but they didn't know how to fight' (quoted in Asher & Hammel 1987: 161).

The second Syrian flaw was leadership. The journalist and military historian Edgar O'Ballance spent some time among the Syrians who fought on the Golan, and his impressions of their officers are worth noting: 'The young officers I saw seemed to be tough, dedicated and keen, but in the middle grades, from major to colonel, I sensed a lack of interest in their profession. The flair and enthusiasm for battle seemed to be absent. Pride prevented them from accepting Soviet advice readily, from admitting mistakes and shortcomings, or taking criticism' (O'Ballance 1979: 343). The poisonous grip of politics on the Syrian officer corps had, if anything, intensified since 1967 now that Hafez al-Assad had forged a stable police state out of Syria's earlier tumultuous decades. Blatant careerism pushed aside much that was sensible and necessary in the interests of personal advancement and expediency.

The men of the Golani Brigade fought in bunkers, from APCs and on foot all across the Golan. Like the rest of the IDF, they were caught off-guard at the outbreak of war in 1973, and especially on the Hermon such surprise cost them dearly. The initial Syrian capture of the outpost in a surprise attack by an augmented battalion of elite soldiers who had trained specifically for the task can hardly be a cause for shame, but the first Israeli attempt to retake the position seemed to expect to succeed through *chutzpah* (audacity) more than planning. Military flair and élan were not enough to carry the day, however, against a more numerous, well-entrenched foe that had the high ground. The second attempt, bloody though it was, did show the initiative, courage and perseverance of the Golani Brigade – the same characteristics that shone through at Outpost 107. It may have been more sensible for the Golani companies to act as a pinning force, however, leaving the recapture of the Hermon to the paratroopers of the 317th who had secured the rear of the mountain with speed and efficiency: they were better positioned to strike at the Syrians on the 'Israeli' Hermon, but it seems that unit pride and a desire to wash away the previous failures dominated the thinking of both the Golani men and the more senior commanders too. Therefore it was bloody frontal attacks rather than tactical flair that carried the day for Israel.

The Israeli soldier was better trained than his Syrian counterpart, but not better armed, and usually outnumbered. Tactical proficiency was immeasurably strengthened by impressive leadership that exhibited bold and adaptable thinking, but probably the most significant element was the fact that to be an Israeli citizen was to be a soldier. The shared understanding of why they served and what was at stake if they failed led to a communal outlook the cohesiveness and sense of purpose of which gave the Israeli soldier his reason to fight.

Aftermath

A team of IDF engineers recover an abandoned Syrian T-54/55 on the Golan, 13 October 1973. As they had done in previous wars, the Israelis made sure not to waste captured equipment and vehicles, with the Soviet T-54, T-55 and (in the wake of the Yom Kippur War) the T-62 taken into IDF service as the TIRAN-4, TIRAN-5 and TIRAN-6 respectively. The tanks underwent varying degrees of internal and external modification that often included new 105mm *Sharir* gun barrels (such models were known as the TIRAN-4Sh and TIRAN-5Sh; the T-62's 115mm gun was deadly enough as it was, requiring no upgrade), American .50- and .30-calibre secondary (machine gun) armament on the turret, new US-made communications gear, as well as a change in their silhouettes (mostly to make them easier to identify from the air) by virtue of the addition of stowage boxes to the hull and turret. (IGPO)

Though talking about the 1956 conflict, Martin van Creveld's observation that it was a case of 'Israel's inability to translate military victory into political achievement' (Creveld 2002: 153) certainly has some resonance with the wars of 1967 and 1973. The Yom Kippur War was very much the child of the Six-Day War, born out of its successes as much as its failures. The 1973 war didn't solve any of the deeper problems that enmeshed the region, but it probably did reduce the chances of new full-scale wars breaking out, and ultimately led to peace between Egypt and Israel through the Camp David Accords of 1978.

The very real rejuvenated pride in Arabic martial prowess was one of the more significant outcomes of the conflict; for Syrians, Egyptians and the wider Arab world, the stain of the 1967 defeats was washed away, the sense of Israeli invincibility broken. Further claims of a renewed sense of Arab identity and purpose that were commonplace soon after the war's conclusion proved to be more expressions of hope than of reality, however.

For Israel the lessons were almost entirely the reverse; the shock of the attacks in Sinai and the Golan, the gossamer-thin closeness with which the Syrians (and to a lesser extent the Egyptians) had come to success, badly shook the Israeli psyche. The nation's unquestioned faith in the supremacy of its armed forces – in spite of what by any measure was a performance of extraordinary skill and bravery – evaporated, and was matched by a growing sense that, buffer zones or not, the armies of their neighbours were not the joke forces they had thought them to be only six years beforehand. Almost as soon as the fighting was over, 'Israelis uniformly [viewed] the war as a type of punishment – in the term coined by former general and president Chaim Herzog, a War of Atonement' (Oren 2013).

Ironically, the renewed confidence within the Arabic societies bled off some of their more overt animus towards their enemy (certainly in Egypt's case), this being matched by the more cautious outlook of the Israelis, who had learned that victory was no guarantee of security. The then-president of Israel, Ephraim Katzir, addressed his nation at the end of the war:

> Between 1967 and 1973 Israel lived in an enchantment. We lived in an imaginary world not related to reality or truth. And it is this psychological condition that is responsible for all the mistakes that happened before the war and during the first few days of it. It has spread in all military, political and social spheres and covered grave weaknesses. All Israelis must know about it and bear its responsibilities. After this terrible war we must learn to be more humble. (Quoted in el Badri et al. 1978: 196–97)

Syrian soldiers, members of the joint Arab 'green helmets' peace-keeping force in Lebanon, atop a Soviet-made tank, November 1976. Though they appear a little rough and ready, their weapons and dress are pretty much the same as they would have been in 1973. Two soldiers carry AK-47 assault rifles (distinguishable from the more modern AKM because the latter sports a distinctive slant-cut muzzle brake), while the man between them has a 7.62mm RPD squad-support light machine gun with a 100-round drum magazine. Note also the *keffiyeh* worn by the cigarette-smoking soldier on the right. (XAVIER BARON/ AFP/Getty Images)

UNIT ORGANIZATIONS

Israeli

By 1967 the 1st 'Golani' Brigade consisted of three mechanized-infantry battalions (the 12th 'Barak', 13th 'Gideon' and 51st 'HaBok'im HaRishon'), as well as a training battalion (the 17th 'Arayot Hagolan'), a mechanized mortar battalion and a reconnaissance company called Sayeret Golani (known as the 'Flying Leopards' thanks to their unit badge). The brigade also had a small engineering and sabotage unit of 50 men which had been established in 1965, squads of which would accompany the main infantry battalions on operations.

An infantry battalion numbered around 650 men at full strength and was comprised of a headquarters company, three rifle companies (each with three platoons) and a support company. The battalions were fully mechanized, the troops being conveyed in the ubiquitous M3 half-tracks (usually armed with FN MAG 58, M1919 or M2 machine guns); by 1973 increasing numbers of the rather unpopular M113 APC were arriving from the United States, but the Golani seem to have stuck with their M3s for the duration of the Yom Kippur War, certainly around the Hermon. The mortar battalion used a mixture of towed 120mm *Soltam* mortars (the prime movers being M3s) and M3 half-tracks with integrated mortar tubes (known as the M3 Mk 'C' for 81mm mortars and M3 Mk 'D' for 120mm mortars) acting as a form of ad hoc self-propelled artillery that proved to be both versatile and effective. There is some confusion as to whether the 1967 establishment included a battery of M3 Mk 'D's with each infantry battalion, but if they were a feature at that time they seem to have been disbanded by 1973.

The Golani infantryman was armed with the FN FAL *Romat* battle rifle, with one man in each squad issued with the heavy-barrelled support version of the *Romat* known as the *Makleon*; squad leaders, officers and vehicle crewmen carried the Uzi submachine gun. Each platoon was supposed to have two bazookas (either an RL-83 Blindicide, M20A1 Super-Bazooka, IMI M20 Super-Bazooka or a captured RPG-7), but most were lucky to have even one. Other personal weapons included Mk 2 'Pineapple' and Mk 26 hand grenades, as well as an anti-tank rifle grenade called the *Rarnat*.

Syrian

The Syrian infantry battalion of 1967 was a variable beast. Though the Syrian Army was slowly modernizing in line with the Soviet model, much of its equipment was outdated and from a variety of sources. Troop transport would be on foot or in trucks, with some of the more mechanized units using BTR-152 armoured personnel carriers.

By 1973, the Syrian motorized-infantry brigade would have three infantry battalions (430 men each) and an associated battalion of tanks (40 strong) with an ATGM and mortar/howitzer battery, as well as various support companies. An infantry battalion would have three companies, each with three 30-man platoons with three squads; all squads would be mounted in APCs (or probably trucks for some second-line troops), with an additional APC serving as the company HQ vehicle. The average squad would be around eight men strong, and would be armed with AKMs or AK-47s, as well as one or two light machine guns (usually the RPD or RPK, but possibly also the heavier PK) and one RPG-7. F1 'Limonka' and RGD-5 grenades would be carried, as would the RKG-3 anti-tank grenade. The infantry would be mounted on BTR-152, BTR-50, BTR-60 and BTR-60PB APCs, sporting a variety of defensive weapons that usually included a 7.62mm machine gun as well as a 12.7mm or 14.5mm weapon. Syria had received around 150–170 BMP-1 infantry fighting vehicles by the outbreak of war.

The 82nd Parachute Battalion, around 500 men strong, had three companies and a command element. It had been trained in reconnaissance, airborne raids by helicopter and parachute, and mountain warfare. Some of its officers had also received special training in the Soviet Union, and the battalion also had access to the best matériel that their Soviet ally had to offer, from the latest small arms (including Dragunov SVD-63 sniper rifles) and night 'scopes to 9M14 *Malyutka* (AT-3) ATGMs and 9K32 *Strela-2* (SA-7) shoulder-launched anti-aircraft missiles. The heavy-weapons company also used the highly portable and effective 82mm B-10 recoilless rifles. The battalion utilized Mi-8 transport helicopters in their attack on the 'Israeli' Hermon, with such assets presumably assigned on an as-needed basis.

BIBLIOGRAPHY

Adler, Larry (1968). 'Melodies on a Harmonica', in Donald Robinson, ed., *Under Fire. Israel's 20-Year Struggle For Survival.* New York, NY: W.W. Norton & Company, pp. 338–41. (Originally published in the *Manchester Guardian Weekly*, 20 July 1967.)

Allon, Yigal (1970). *The Making of Israel's Army.* London: Valentine, Mitchell & Co. Ltd.

Asher, Jerry & Hammel, Eric M. (1987). *Duel for the Golan: the 100-hour battle that saved Israel.* Pacifica, CA: Pacifica Military History.

Blum, Howard (2004). *The Eve of Destruction: The Untold Story of the Yom Kippur War.* New York, NY: Harper Perennial.

Bowen, Jeremy (2004). *Six Days: How the 1967 War Shaped the Middle East.* London: Simon & Schuster.

Brant, Bruce A. (1986). *Battlefield Air Interdiction in the 1973 Middle East War and its Significance to NATO Air Operations.* US Army Command and General Staff College, Kansas. Available online at: http://www.dtic.mil/cgi-bin/GetTRDoc?Location=U2&doc=GetTRDoc.pdf&AD=ADA186417 (accessed 11 August 2014).

Creveld, Martin van (2002). *The Sword and the Olive: A Critical History of the Israeli Defense Force.* New York, NY: Public Affairs.

Dunstan, Simon (2008). *Israeli Fortifications of the October War 1973.* Fortress 79. Oxford: Osprey Publishing.

Dunstan, Simon (2009). *The Six Day War 1967: Jordan and Syria.* Campaign 216. Oxford: Osprey Publishing.

el Badri, Hassan, el Magdoub, Taha & el Din Zohdy, Mohammed Dia (1978). *The Ramadan War, 1973.* Dunn Loring, VA: T.N. Dupuy Associates Inc. (First published in Arabic in 1974 by United Company for Publishing and Distribution, Cairo.)

Fogelman, Shay (2010). *Druze residents of the Golan Heights, who had served in the Syrian army, reminisce about the Six-Day War.* Available online at: http://www.haaretz.co.il/misc/1.1198627 (accessed 20 December 2015).

Gal, Reuven (1986). *A Portrait of the Israeli Soldier.* Contributions in Military Studies. Westport, CT: Greenwood Press.

Hashavia, Arye, trans. from the Hebrew by Bina Gershuni, Frances Kay & David Saraph (1969). *A History of the Six-Day War.* Tel-Aviv: Ledory Publishing House.

Herzog, Chaim (1982). *The Arab-Israeli Wars: War and Peace in the Middle East.* New York, NY: Random House.

Khalidi, Ahmed S. (1975). 'The Military Balance, 1967–73', in Arui, Naseer H., ed., *Middle East Crucible: Studies on the Arab–Israeli War of October 1973.* Wilmette, IL: Medina University Press International, pp. 21–63.

Kober, Avi (2011). 'The Rise and Fall of Israeli Operational Art, 1948–2008', in John Andreas Olsen & Martin van Creveld (eds), *The Evolution of Operational Art: From Napoleon to the Present.* Oxford: Oxford University Press, pp. 166–94.

Kotas-Bar, Chen (2013). *Outpost Portugal.* (Originally published in Hebrew in the newspaper *Maariv*, 14 September 2013.) Available online at: http://www.yadlashiryon.com/show_item.asp?levelId=63829&itemId=5290 (accessed 10 September 2015).

Luttwak, Edward & Horowitz, Dan (1975). *The Israeli Army.* London: Allen Lane.

Mauldin, Bill (1968). 'War on a Shoestring', in Donald Robinson, ed., *Under Fire. Israel's 20-Year Struggle For Survival.* New York, NY: W.W. Norton & Co., pp. 335–37.

Nicolle, David & Cooper, Tom (2004). *Arab MiG-19 and MiG-21 Units in Combat.* Combat Aircraft 44. Oxford: Osprey Publishing.

O'Ballance, Edgar (1979). *No Victor, No Vanquished: the Yom Kippur War.* London: Barrie & Jenkins.

Oren, Michael B. (2002). *Six Days of War: June 1967 and the Making of the Modern Middle East.* Oxford: Oxford University Press.

Oren, Michael B. (2013). 'The Yom Kippur War at 40 – A Look Back', in *New Republic*, 15 October 2013. Available online at: www.newrepublic.com/article/115154/yom-kippur-war-40-look-back (accessed 7 August 2014).

Pollack, Kenneth M. (2004). *Arabs at War: Military Effectiveness, 1948–1991.* Lincoln, NE: University of Nebraska Press. (First published 2002.)

Prosch, Geoffrey G. (1979). 'Israeli Defense of the Golan: an Interview with Brigadier General Avigdor Kahalani', in *Military Review*, October 1979: 2–13. Available online at: http://cgsc.cdmhost.com/cdm/singleitem/collection/p124201coll1/id/364/rec/1 (accessed 11 August 2014).

Rabinovich, Abraham (2004). *The Yom Kippur War: The Epic Encounter That Transformed the Middle East.* New York, NY: Schocken Books.

Rothenberg, Gunther E. (1979). *The Anatomy of the Israeli Army.* London: Batsford.

Segev, Tom, trans. Jessica Cohen (2007). *1967: Israel, the War, and the Year that Transformed the Middle East.* London: Abacus. (Originally published in Israel in 2005 under the title *1967: Vehaaretz shinta et paneiha* by Keter Publishers, Jerusalem.)

Shaked, Gideon (2014). *The Battle on Mount Hermon in the Yom Kippur War of 1973 – The courage of the Golani soldiers under fire.* Available online at: http://www.onjewishmatters.com/who-are-the-golani-soldiers-the-battle-on-mount-hermon-in-the-yom-kippur-war-of-1973 (accessed 20 August 2015).

Shoufani, Elias (1975). 'The October War and the Israeli Press', in Naseer H. Arui, ed., *Middle East Crucible: Studies on the Arab-Israeli War of October 1973.* Wilmette, IL: Medina University Press International, pp. 173–97.

Sunday Times Insight Team (1974). *The Yom Kippur War.* New York, NY: Doubleday & Co.

Wakebridge, Charles (1976). 'The Syrian Side of the Hill', in *Military Review*, February 1976: 20–30 Available online at: http://cgsc.cdmhost.com/cdm/singleitem/collection/p124201coll1/id/331/rec/1 (accessed 11 August 2014).

Weller, Jac (1974). 'Sir Basil Liddell Hart's Disciples in Israel', in *Military Review*, January 1974: 13–23. Available online at: http://cgsc.cdmhost.com/cdm/singleitem/collection/p124201coll1/id/390/rec/2 (accessed 8 August 2014).

Weller, Jac (1977). 'Armor and Infantry in Israel', in *Military Review*, April 1977: 3–11. Available online at: http://cgsc.cdmhost.com/cdm/singleitem/collection/p124201coll1/id/381/rec/1 (accessed 8 August 2014).

INDEX

References to illustrations are shown in **bold**.
References to plates are shown in bold with
caption pages in brackets, e.g. **38–39**, (40).